MW01231701

Published by
John L. Betcher
Red Wing, Minnesota
www.johnbetcher.com
john@johnbetcher.com
2010

ISBN:1453833250
EAN-13: 9781453833254

A HIGHER COURT

COURT

One Man's Search for the Truth
of God's Existence

by

John L. Betcher

As the coming storm stalks the unwary, so Truth pursues me. If I turn to the right, he will find me. If I turn to the left, he will seek me out. The only way to flee is forward.

When I reach the edge of the abyss, Truth will overtake me. He will bear me across the depths . . . or shove me in.

William L. Kensey

Prologue

My name is William Kensey. I have a wife and two great kids. Until very recently, I was a well-respected and financially successful trial attorney.

I was also a man who was comfortable with his religion. I preferred it served at arm's length from the pulpit on Sunday morning. And would rather not discuss it the rest of the week.

The circumstances that led me to write A HIGHER COURT changed all that. The entire experience was both bizarre and unavoidable. You see, I was summoned to serve as a juror in an improbable trial -- a trial to determine whether God exists.

I know.

You think that sounds ludicrous. I did, too . . . until the trial began.

Witnesses buried me under mountains of scientific evidence. My own eyes forced me to confront the reality of extreme human suffering. God seemed less and less relevant -- even absent -- as the trial progressed.

At the close of the trial, I had to render my verdict -- "God" or "No God." Affirm a new and deeper faith in a Creator, or confess the triumph of science.

A HIGHER COURT is the story of how I discovered the ultimate truth. I invite you to join me in this revelation. You won't be sorry.

CHAPTER 1
DAD'S DEATH

I couldn't really blame the soccer mom for ending my father's life. While she sat at the wheel of her SUV, her fourth-grade son bludgeoned her third-grade daughter with his shin pad in the back seat, causing a momentary distraction. That was all it had taken for her to miss seeing Dad step into the crosswalk.

The accident could have happened to anyone. It just turned out to be Dad.

Better him than a father of young children. One could give thanks for that much. My siblings and I were all middle-aged. Dad was 74. We could as easily have lost him to a heart attack or stroke. He was a heavy smoker, after all. As fate would have it, it was this poor woman's truck that had claimed his life.

My family had already learned there is never a good time for death. We'd lost Mom to cancer a few years ago. The ordeal had been agony. Her dying was a prolonged and painful process. Not like Dad's. At least Dad hadn't suffered.

But swift or slow, death is unpleasant, whenever and wherever it happens.

We held Dad's visitation at the funeral home the evening before we planned to bury his body. My siblings and I (two sisters and myself – the sole surviving male in the Kensey family) stood in the receiving line, shaking hands and exchanging hugs with well-wishers. We spared our children the ordeal of joining in that ritual. They gathered in a separate suite of rooms at the funeral home, exchanging Grandpa stories with their cousins.

No one is comfortable on either side of a funeral receiving line.

There really isn't a 'right' thing to say to the family. Or a correct response either. Standing until your feet ache, and robotically hugging near-total strangers, is just part of the dying process. It must be done.

Lined up for hours, we heard some of the more common condolences many times over.

"I'm sorry for your loss."

"He was such a good man. It's a shame he died so young."

"You have our sincerest sympathy. Is there anything we can do? Maybe bring over lasagna?"

And then there was the occasional fool who insisted on explaining Dad's death to us.

"I know you'll miss him. But I'm sure it's for the best. It must be part of God's plan."

'God's plan.' What I wouldn't give to have a clue as to what 'God's plan' was. Whatever plan God had in mind, I'm pretty sure Dad getting run over by a two-ton vehicle on a sunny afternoon wasn't part of it. Nor the life-long guilt the young mother at the wheel would suffer.

'God's plan.' What a crock!

The funeral was held the morning after the visitation at the Lutheran church I had grown up in, and of which Dad was still a member at his death. The place was packed with folks paying their last respects. Dad was a well-liked guy.

The minister offered moving words about my father from the pulpit. He was a "good man, a loving husband and father, and a child of God." He spoke for quite a while. But I was distracted – unprepared to focus on a sermon today.

When the minister had finished, I delivered the eulogy.

Standing there, a middle-aged man in a black lawyer's suit, I grasped both sides of the pulpit and hung my head. Rotating my well-coiffed graying hair solemnly side to side, I prepared to speak.

Most congregants probably thought I was praying. Actually, I was just setting the proper mood for the eulogy I was about to present.

My eulogy was short. But it hit the high points of my father's existence. I shared anecdotes extolling the great husband, father and grandfather Dad had been through the years. There were some tears from the mourners when I mentioned Mom's death.

When it came time to lighten the mood, I produced a large, green zucchini squash and laid it on the pulpit in plain view. There was laughter when I reminded everyone how Dad had forcibly shared his bountiful zucchini harvest with every sorry soul unfortunate enough to pass by his garden when the crop was at its peak.

After the service, the immediate family attended the committal at the cemetery. Oakwood would normally be a beautiful and peaceful place to visit on a late August morning. Today, I would rather have stood almost anywhere else.

'Ashes to ashes. Dust to dust.'

Yeah, yeah, yeah. So I see. Is that all there is to it? Really?

We watched Dad's casket descend into the rectangular hole in the warm brown earth. My sisters sobbed. Some of the grandkids ran around the cemetery, playing tag among the elms. Others stood, shell-shocked at the grave side.

No one wanted to throw the first shovelful of dirt on Dad. So the reverend just gave us all his blessings and wished us well.

The committal was over. We were off to the reception back in the church fellowship hall.

As I rode in the rear of a black limo with my wife and two somber daughters, I wondered why I wasn't feeling more emotional about Dad's passing. I had loved him, certainly. Shouldn't his death make me sad, or angry, or something?

I just felt numb.

And where was he now? In heaven?

That's what I'd been taught through years of Lutheran upbringing. He had 'ascended' and was with his 'Heavenly Father.' I think my trouble believing all the memorized dogma was that, as a lawyer, I have both an innate skepticism of anything unprovable, and a tendency to remain vigilant for ways any circumstance can go wrong. Those traits certainly benefit my clients. They were not helpful to me today.

I *hoped* Dad had gone to heaven. But I was far from sure of it. He might just be . . . dead.

Frankly, I felt more compassion for the unfortunate woman who had killed Dad, than I did grief over Dad's death itself. What was wrong with me? Or was this just the way things are . . . the way they should be?

When we arrived back at the church, the pastor must have sensed my ambivalence. He pulled me aside to ask if I was okay.

"Sure."

"You seem distracted . . . distant. Is there any way I can help?"

"I don't think so Reverend. I'm good. I mean, I'm all right under the circumstances."

"Are you sure I couldn't say a prayer with you? Ask for God's peace for you and your family?"

"Ah . . . go ahead and say that prayer, Reverend. But I think I need to be with my wife and kids right now."

"As you wish. God bless you."

"You, too. Gotta go."

Praying and preaching and church etiquette had always given me the creeps. The *last* thing I wanted to do was hold some preacher's hand while he prayed for me. The thought sent shivers down my spine. I beat a hasty retreat to the safety of the mourning throng.

Dad was dead. Wasn't that bad enough? Should I have to confront religious zealots as well? I didn't think so.

Later that night, after the kids had retreated to their rooms, my wife, Jen, asked how I was doing.

"Fine. How 'bout you?"

"I'm okay, Hon," she said. "I'm just a little worried about you, that's all. You seemed a little . . . distant . . . today."

"Jen. I'm sort of surprised how ill-at-ease I felt with the church ceremonies, the out-pouring of emotions from Dad's friends and the whole 'ritual' of it all. I'm Lutheran, am I not? It shouldn't have seemed so . . . weird. Should it?

"I mean, if funerals are supposed to be for the deceased's family, I don't see why. I probably wouldn't have gone to the funeral at all if people didn't expect me to be there."

Jen slid over, nuzzling her head on my chest as we sat on the couch.

"I'm sorry," she said.

"Sorry for what?" I asked without emotion.

"Sorry your faith hasn't brought you comfort today."

I took a deep breath and exhaled slowly.

"I imagine that my 'faith,' or lack of it, is likely at the root of my discomfort. I'll work my way through it. You don't need to worry. I'm a grown man, you know. I can deal with these things."

"I love you," Jen said.

"You too, Jen. So . . . how about we turn in? I'm beat."

CHAPTER 2
THE SUMMONS

The morning after Dad's funeral was a Saturday. I hadn't slept well and awoke at 6:00 a.m. My lack of distress over Dad's death still troubled me. I brewed some coffee and sat in the living room to read yesterday's paper, which remained largely untouched.

Jen and the kids were still sleeping when the mail arrived at 9:00.

As I stood in my slippers and robe leafing through the usual collection of magazines, bills and junk mail, one item stood out. The business-size envelope was made of heavy linen stock and gleamed a bright white. In the upper left corner, the return address proclaimed: 'United States District Court, District of Minnesota.' An official-looking seal dominated the back flap. The letter was addressed to William Laurence Kensey and marked: 'OPEN IMMEDIATELY. DATED MATERIAL.'

Tossing the rest of the mailbox contents on the kitchen table, I slit the top of the envelope open with my forefinger and slid out the single sheet of white paper inside.

A Jury Summons. The Federal Court was calling me for jury duty.

The Summons instructed me to appear at the seventh floor Clerk of Court's Office in the United States Federal Courthouse, downtown Minneapolis, a week from this coming Monday at 8:00 a.m.

Initially, I was irritated at the impending disruption to my work schedule. Then I decided that the day off from work, cloistered with a jury pool of strangers, might actually give me a chance to sort out my feelings about Dad's death in silence . . . and without having someone pestering to pray with me.

A familiar sound interrupted my contemplation.

"Good morning, Daddy," my daughters sang in unison as they skipped down the stairs, still wearing their summer PJs, their voices cheerful with the new day.

"Morning girls."

"What's for breakfast?" sixteen year old Annie asked, glancing at the void on the kitchen table, and sounding a bit disenfranchised. Annie was a slender blonde, like her mother. Meticulous and bright, she was a model student. She had reached the age where her parents' collective IQ was in free fall – but she usually put up with us in a respectful manner.

"Anybody want pancakes?" I asked, tucking the Summons into my robe pocket. The girls' favorite breakfast.

"Yay!"

"Okay. I'll tell you what. If you two will go out to the garden and pick some flowers for your mother, I'll get the griddle going."

"Deal," twelve-year-old Shannon called, heading for the patio doors.

Shannon favored my Irish blood. All red hair and freckles, she was full of questions, and could be stubborn as hell. I was sure this latter trait would serve her well one day . . . but for right now, it often made her a handful. She had embraced the flower project though. So out the door they both went.

Twenty minutes later, Jen had arisen, and all four of us Kenseys were gathered around the breakfast table. We said grace, after which the kids attacked the stack of pancakes like a pride of starving lions. Jen and I smiled at each other. Neither of us was a big breakfast eater. We each took a single cake, leaving extras in case the kids wanted seconds.

The girls had collected a bouquet of late-blooming tulips, which Annie had arranged precisely in a tall, clear vase and displayed on the table.

After Shannon had stuffed her mouth with pancake drenched in maple syrup, she stood up and plucked one of the tulips from the vase.

Annie expressed irritation.

"Dad, Shannon just messed up the flowers. Those flowers are for Mom."

"It's all right, Annie. Mom doesn't mind." I glanced at Jen, who was shaking her head in agreement. "And they still look beautiful."

Annie gave her younger sister a dirty look.

"And Shannon, what's up with the flower pilfering?"

"Daddy look." She held out the tulip toward me. "This one has two flowers instead of one. It's special."

Shannon was, of course, correct. The flower she held was an oddity. Unlike the other tulips in the vase, the one in her hand had grown a second blossom, which protruded oddly from its oval stem.

"Why does this one have two flowers instead of just one, like the others?" Shannon wanted to know.

Her frown demanded an answer.

"It's a mutant," Annie jumped in. "Its DNA is screwed up. It's a freak flower." Annie seemed to take just a smidgen of pleasure in deriding her sister's discovery.

"Hey! Hey! Hey! It is not a 'freak flower.' " I glanced purposefully at Annie, who lowered her head a tiny bit. "It's just different, that's all," I said toward Shannon. "God made it that way."

Jen and I had been using the 'God made it that way' answer with the girls all their lives. It generally defused an endless series of 'why' questions.

"But, Dad," Annie objected, "that's not true. That stem is supposed to only have one flower on it. We learned it in biology. It probably started out normal and something happened to its DNA. So now it's a mutant," she said, flicking a glance at Shannon.

Parenting had become more challenging as the girls got older. Jen smiled through a sip from her coffee mug, peering at me over its rim to see what I would say next.

"My flower is *not* a mutant! Tell her, Daddy."

"I don't think we need to blow this out of proportion, girls. Maybe something changed the flower to make it grow this way. But maybe God made that something happen. Seems to me that two blossoms *are* better than one." I was pretty pleased with the cleverness of my solution.

"That's not how it works, Dad." Annie wasn't satisfied. "The flower DNA starts out as a perfect blueprint to grow the flower," she recited. "Then something like nuclear radiation, or chemicals, or . . . or flower mutant disease made it into a *mutant*! God doesn't make mutants."

Annie and Shannon exchanged looks that could easily have been accompanied by protruding tongues.

I wasn't prepared to get into the details of Darwin's theory of evolution at the breakfast table.

"But, Annie," I said. "Maybe God wanted to make this flower special, and He used the chemicals in insecticides or fertilizer to help Him do the job."

Annie looked doubtful.

"We could go back and forth on this for hours," Jen said. "You girls are done eating. Put your dishes in the dishwasher, please. Then go find something fun to do outside. It's too beautiful a day to be inside arguing."

Both girls complied.

When the dishes were in the washer, Shannon grasped her special flower by the stem, skipped out of the room and headed up the stairs, sing-song taunting as she went – "God made me a flower. God made me a flower."

Annie followed close behind. "You're both mutants!"

The girls were gone. Jen smiled at me. We finished our coffee in peace.

CHAPTER 3
THE VOLLEYBALL TOURNAMENT

Exactly one week after the 'mutant flower incident,' as Jen and I had come to refer to it, another Saturday morning rolled around – just as the calendar had predicted. But today was not a day for thoughts of genetic anomalies, or pondering Grandpa's death. This day promised excitement and heightened emotions for the entire Kensey family . . . and for St. Paul's Academy as well.

Perhaps it's an overstatement to say that all of St. Paul's would be excited about today. But certainly its volleyball players were wound up.

Today was the day of our athletic conference's pre-season tournament. All sixteen of the conference schools would be there, vying for the early honor of "Conference Tournament Champion."

Particularly on edge would be a B-Squad outside hitter named Annie Kensey, and her father, the team's Coach. I'm sure other players and parents shared in the excitement. I *know* we felt it acutely at our house.

To understand the context of this tournament, and its import to the teams involved, one needs to know a few things about our school and the East Minnie Conference.

St. Paul's is a 250 student, grade nine through twelve, non-denominational Christian school where we had enrolled Annie, not for its religious roots, but for the quality of education it offered. St. Paul's had a long-standing reputation for turning out top college academic candidates. Not so much for grooming college athletes or ministers.

Most schools in the East Minnie had roughly the same enrollment as St. Paul's. In other words, the conference name reflected not only its presence in Minnesota, but also the tiny size of its constituent institutions. The thought of playing a volleyball team from the East Minnie didn't exactly put the fear of God into most opponents.

Annie and I had been involved in volleyball since she joined a club team at age ten. I wasn't much of a volleyball guru at the time. But I volunteered to assist the team's coach, who frankly, knew little more about volleyball than I.

In those early years, I memorized the volleyball rule book, and got my hands on every youth coaching text I could find. I began networking with more advanced and knowledgeable coaches – picking their brains for valuable insights. I even earned an advanced volleyball coaching certificate from USA Volleyball . . . the Olympic volleyball folks.

In short – and in keeping with my compulsive reluctance to perform any task 'half-way' – over the course of Annie's five years of playing the sport, I had become a highly over-qualified youth volleyball coach.

When I asked St. Paul's if they would consider allowing me to coach Annie's teams in school ball, they were happy to have my assistance for the unpaid, and predominantly revolving-door, position.

All of which leads us to this Saturday's Tournament.

Although not meaningful in the scheme of state competitions, regional titles, or even 'official' conference records, the tournament had taken on an outsized importance to its participants. It was a battle to be the big frog in the little puddle – at least for one day. And for the B Squad teams . . . a less big frog in an even tinier puddle.

But it was *our* puddle, nevertheless.

The B Squad Tournament was to be held in the Scottfield High gym. Our team arrived early, as I had requested. And by the time of our first contest, we were ready to play.

Being avid volleyball fans, Jen and Shannon were always present in the bleachers, cheering their heads off for St. Paul's.

Our first victory came easily. The opposition struggled to even return our serves. This caliber of play was not uncommon in the East Minnie. Sometimes the team that was able to put its serves in play was able to win the day on the basis of that skill alone. (That's partly why, at St. Paul's, we focused a good deal on serving in practice.)

The Tournament proceeded throughout the day. The cream puffs had been eliminated in the first round. Subsequent matches required every bit of playing and coaching skills our team could bring to bear.

Partly because of team effort and execution, and partly owing to fortuity, St. Paul's advanced through the tournament to the semi-final round. Just four teams left out of a field of sixteen.

It was at the beginning of the semi-final match that I couldn't avoid noticing the arrival on site of a late-coming parent of one of my players. John Lester was a surly fellow, known more for his candor than his socially appropriate delivery of the same.

Early in the first set I could hear his grumblings from the bleachers. He wanted more playing time for his daughter, Kaitlen.

From the bench, using face and hand gestures, Kait tried to shush him. But he refused to be shushed. With the passing of each set, his presence in the stands became more and more pronounced.

Toward the end of the last set, he was yelling at me to "For God's sake, coach. Let 'er play."

He was correct that his daughter was not getting a lot of playing time during this tournament. But Kait understood why and was okay with it.

One of the skills I had acquired early in my coaching career was clear communication with players and parents. Each season, I went out of my way to explain my coaching philosophy – both orally at a player-parent meeting, and then again in a writing sent home with each player. Mr. Lester did not attend the meeting.

These communications reinforced my philosophy that life lessons are more important than volleyball skills.

We had five team rules. Every year they were the same.

1) Show Respect.
2) Communicate Positively.
3) Try.
4) Make Mistakes.
5) No walking in the practice gym.

Players would receive court time in matches based on their adherence to the above five rules, and their 'readiness to play.'

Unless a player had committed a serious violation (e.g. repeatedly missing practice; using drugs or alcohol; fighting; disrupting practices, etc.), every player would receive appropriate playing time in every match.

All the players knew these rules well, since I reinforced them – by complimenting appropriate behaviors – at every practice.

Unlike nearly all of the other players on our team, who were serious about improving their volleyball skills, Kaitlen's involvement in the program was mainly social. At our team's level of volleyball expertise – and given the players' young ages – Kaitlen's motivations were, in my mind, entirely appropriate.

But since she did little to comply with the team rules at practice . . . especially the 'Try' rule . . . I had told her only two days ago about the limited role she would play in today's matches. She indicated her understanding and assured me that she would pass this information along to her parents – which may or may not have happened.

Back at the tournament, St. Paul's managed to win our semi-final match, despite Mr. Lester's distracting behavior. The team was ecstatic.

Now we had an hour-long break while the other semi-final contestants battled it out. I congratulated the girls on their stellar performances on the volleyball court. Then instructed them to relax, drink something and have a light snack, whether they were thirsty or hungry or not.

We broke from our game-end huddle. The players went their

ways, and I found a table where I could plan out lineups and strategies for our next match.

Not surprisingly, Mr. Lester sought me out.

I saw his hulking frame approaching and stood to greet him.

"Good afternoon, Mr. Lester. Good to see you. I'm glad you were able to make it for our final two matches."

I extended my hand to shake.

He scowled, brushing my hand aside brusquely.

"Who the Hell do you think you are?" he said in a hushed tone.

"I beg your pardon?" I responded, calmly. "I'm your daughter's coach."

"Don't be a smart-ass with me, Boy. Kaitlen hardly played at all in that last match. This is kid's volleyball for God's sake. They should all get to play."

It was apparent that logic was not going to help me deal with Mr. Lester. I took a step closer to Mr. Lester, just to let him know I wasn't intimidated.

Not wishing to create a scene, my voice was also quiet.

"Kaitlen plays. And her playing time is exactly what I promised it would be at the beginning of the season. I'm sorry if you're unhappy with the situation. But grousing to me isn't going to change anything."

It appeared that Mr. Lester's negotiation arsenal was limited to intimidation tactics. This was understandable given his considerable size.

"Don't give me that shit! I expect to see Kaitlen on that court *at least* as much as any other player this next match, or I'll have you thrown out as coach. You got it?"

Mr. Lester didn't appreciate that, since I was an unpaid volunteer, his having me removed as coach, if he could do it, would not be a grave inconvenience to me.

"I understand your position, Mr. Lester." My voice was still quiet. And I kept my temper under control. "Now please, allow me to plan my rotations and prepare for our next match."

Mr. Lester wasn't sure if he'd accomplished his goal or not. But parents and players were beginning to look our way. And he decided to break off the confrontation.

He turned abruptly and took a seat at the table where Kaitlen's mother sat red-faced with embarrassment.

Jen came over to check on me.

"Problems?" she asked.

"Nothing to be concerned about. Just a parent wanting more playing time for his kid. It'll be okay."

Jen returned to a table where the other volleyball mothers were laughing and snacking. I continued my pre-match preparations.

When it was time for us to return to the court for the championship match, we went through our warmups as usual. I noticed Mr. Lester in the front row of the bleachers, arms crossed and defiant.

I waved at Jen and Shannon and gave them a thumbs-up.

As the players continued their warmups, the referees conducted the coin toss and I returned to our team bench to fill out the pre-match paperwork.

My initial lineup took the floor. It did not include Kaitlen, who remained, for now, on the bench with me, as she had at the beginning of every prior set. Shannon happened to be on the bench as well.

Just when I was hoping that we would survive the day without further interference from Mr. Lester, he hefted his bulk off the bleachers and strode across the court, coming to a dead stop right in front of me . . . and his daughter.

I glanced at Kait. Her head was hanging.

I stood.

"Mr. Lester. You need to leave the playing area so we can start the set."

Again his voice was hushed. "I'm not moving one foot 'til I see my daughter out there on that court."

"Then we've got a problem, sir. Because the referee is not going to start the match with you standing on the court."

"Then you'd better fix it! Put her on the damn court!"

Mr. Lester's level of belligerence is exceedingly rare in the genteel sport of volleyball. And I had never before had a parent who was uncooperative to this extent. But I had an idea.

"I am asking you politely, Mr. Lester. Please leave the court and sit down."

He crossed his arms and gave me an angry stare.

I plucked my rule book from my coach's bag and left Mr. Lester standing by the team bench.

Since our confrontation had already garnered the attention of the opposing coach, she also stood and joined me at the referee's stand. The three of us discussed the situation in muted tones.

"My apologies to both of you," I said. "I have an obstinate and irate parent on my hands. And he won't leave the court."

I went on to explain the whole situation.

At first the referee was flustered. He had never encountered these circumstances either.

"Well, what am I supposed to do about it?" he said. "I don't have authority to throw out a spectator."

"Please," I said. "I think I have a solution."

I handed the referee my rule book with it opened to the appropriate page.

"According to the rules, you can throw out a coach who fails to control his team's fans," I said. "Give me a warning and then we'll see if you need to throw me out."

The opposing coach had been listening with her head bowed. She looked up at my suggestion.

"But Coach," the referee said, "if I toss you, your team won't have a coach and will have to forfeit this match."

"I recognize that."

The referee turned to the opposing coach.

"How do you feel about this, Coach? It's a pretty bizarre situation and I want us all to be on the same page here," the referee said.

"My team would much rather play than win by forfeit. We'd

cream you anyway." She smiled at me. "But I respect Mr. Kensey's willingness to stand by his principles. I'm okay whichever way this goes."

She turned to me. "Good luck."

"Okay," I said. "Ref, please give me a yellow card for unsportsmanlike conduct on my parent's behalf. Then I'll do what I can to resolve this stalemate. If my plan doesn't work . . . well . . . you'll have one less match to officiate today."

The referee nodded. The coaches returned to their benches. Mr. Lester stayed put.

The referee pulled a yellow plastic card from his back pocket and held it up for the teams and audience to see.

"Unsportsmanlike conduct, St. Paul's Coach." He made a 'C' with his other hand as he held both arms aloft.

"One point will be awarded to Scottfield."

A '1' appeared in the 'Home' column on the scoreboard.

I could see Jen and Shannon looking concerned in the bleachers.

"What's goin' on?" Mr. Lester demanded. "What's the deal with giving the other team a point before the game's even started?"

"That's the least of our problems," I said, looking the big man in the eye.

"If you don't vacate not only this court, but the entire building immediately, I will be ejected from the game."

Mr. Lester grinned. "That'd be fine with me."

"And our team would forfeit this match."

The grin disappeared.

"According to the rules, a team can't play without a *certified* coach on its bench. There's not another *certified* coach here to replace me. So if I get tossed, we lose."

Mr. Lester turned toward the referee, who now held both a yellow and a red card in his hand, and was looking questioningly my way.

Poor Kait, who had been sitting on the bench right in front of the entire confrontation, began bawling uncontrollably. Shannon put an arm around Kait's shoulders.

Mr. Lester looked at his daughter . . . then at the referee, who was wiggling the cards impatiently . . . then back at me.

"Okay. You win."

"Make sure to leave the building," I said, before Mr. Lester departed. "If you're seen anywhere inside the venue, we forfeit the match."

He growled at me. But he left.

The teams were ready, and the referee blew the whistle to begin the match.

Shannon and I did our best to comfort Kait as she sat next to us on the bench during the first few points of that set.

"Breathe. In . . . and . . . out. I need you to collect yourself so you can play when your turn comes around," I said.

She looked up at me.

"You're still going to play me after all that with my dad?" Her red eyes were incredulous.

"Sure. Not your fault. You should meet my dad some day." I smiled. "He would really scare you."

I laughed to myself at the thought of Kait meeting Dad's ghost. There was a fleeting twinge in my gut. And then it was gone.

Both teams played their hearts out in that Championship Match. The lead changed hands frequently. Each team had won two sets when the fifth, and final, set began.

First team to fifteen wins.

After struggling during the opening rallies, we found ourselves trailing Scottfield 13 - 9 when we finally regained the serve. We needed to score six points before they scored two. It was a formidable challenge.

To make my choices more difficult, our next server was none other than Kaitlen. She was an average server at best. Strictly playing the odds, with Kaitlen's service record, I could reasonably have conceded the game to Scottfield right then and there.

I had my best server on the bench. My daughter, Annie. I could have subbed her in for Kaitlen. And believe me, I wanted to do just that. I was sure the rest of my team – and probably a lot of parents as well – would have approved of the substitution.

But I remembered the team rules and my coaching philosophy. *Life is more important than volleyball.* I had to repeat it to myself.

I thought about how Kaitlen might feel being pulled from the game at this juncture. Maybe she would be relieved. Or more likely, disheartened.

No. I would not deprive Kait of her chance to serve – whatever the results might be on the court.

Kait looked at me tentatively as she rotated to the server's spot. *Would I pull her?*

I gave her a thumbs up and a big smile.

She smiled back.

I could relay the details of that match's ending. But suffice it to say that St. Paul's won the Championship by a score of 15 - 13. And Kait?

She never missed a serve.

CHAPTER 4
THE COURT

On the morning of the trial I awoke at 4:30 to the crack of lightning, followed closely by a deep rumble of thunder. A moment later, pouring rain rattled our tile roof. I rolled over in bed, hoping for another hour or two of rest.

As I drifted in and out of sleep, unfounded worries dogged my semi-conscious mind. Bizarre concerns that I would, for some inexplicable reason, be unable to reach a verdict. That the evidence would confuse me. That I would fail, somehow, to reach the correct outcome.

After an hour of tossing and turning, I was fully awake and atypically nervous. I could write off the dreams I'd experienced during the storm to pre-trial adrenaline – a state I'd often experienced before trying a case. Or it may have been due to the unfamiliar role I would play as juror in the court proceedings to be held that day. Whatever the reason, I remained anxious and uneasy all the way through my solo breakfast.

On the way to the courthouse, the pouring rain increased in intensity as I drove toward downtown. Shallow lakes formed on the freeway, bringing traffic to a crawl. Wipers slashed with futility across the windshield, barely interrupting the grey-green impressionist landscapes cascading downward before me. I couldn't remember the last time it had rained this hard. The extended commute and darkened skies did nothing to lift my somber mood.

By the time I had arrived at the Courthouse, it was 7:45. Ramp parking and a skyway passage to the courthouse allowed me to stay dry despite the deluge.

Walking the familiar halls to the designated room, I began to hit my stride . . . so to speak. The peculiar malaise that had beset me earlier was beginning to lift. There's nothing like the comfort of familiar surroundings to ease the mind.

As I approached the assigned door, my complete focus returned to the here and now.

The eye-level sign read: 'Jury Assembly.' I knew this place from my experience as a trial lawyer. We would gather here to await further instructions from the Court.

I turned the knob and leaned into the heavy, metal door.

Inside the room, a few prospective jurors were already seated in the shiny black metal chairs that lined its perimeter. Each kept to him- or her-self.

I pulled out a heavy wooden chair from one of the large oak tables anchoring the center of the space, sat down and laid my morning newspaper, still folded, in front of me. No one spoke. Heads were bowed and hands crossed on laps. Most avoided eye contact with others.

I took a deep breath and closed my eyes. The sounds and smells of this courthouse, even this room, comforted and assured me. This was my venue . . . my home away from home. I had won and lost many trials here. Truth be told, every verdict had, at least to my mind, been the right one under the circumstances. I was capable of extreme objectivity in such evaluations. Of course, I was not in the practice of sharing my after-the-fact assessments with unsuccessful clients.

I picked up the paper and tried to catch up on world events. Jurors continued to file in.

I caught myself grinning into the newsprint. I had been correct in my assumption that no one had offered to pray with me.

As 8:00 approached, the lights in the Assembly Room suddenly went dark . . . an apparent power failure. There should have been an emergency light. But there wasn't. Since this room had no windows, everything was black as tar.

Someone had the good sense to call out, "Stay where you are. I'm sure the lights will be back on shortly."

All was now quiet, dark and still. The air was thick with human breath and perspiration. My eyes tried to focus, but to no avail. I was beginning to feel disoriented in the blackness. The sense of unease I had felt earlier crept back into my consciousness.

Then, just as quickly as they had gone off, the ceiling fluorescents flickered on, flooding the room with a startling brightness.

After my eyes had recovered from the lighting change, I noticed that a uniformed gentleman now stood in a doorway opposite the door through which I had entered. Pudgy and geriatric, his uniform indicated that he was a Court Officer of some sort. Probably the Bailiff.

I couldn't tell whether he had arrived before the light, or while my eyes were adjusting. In any event, I hadn't seen him come in.

I laid my paper on the table and waited. Eventually, everyone noticed the Officer. The room fell silent. All awaited whatever announcement the Officer was sure to make.

Holding a pencil and clipboard, he surveyed the room, referencing a checklist of some sort as he did so. It was all a matter of routine. A ritual . . . not unlike Dad's funeral proceedings. A *sine qua non* – a prerequisite – before proceeding to the next step in the trial process.

After a moment, the chubby gentleman announced, "All who were expected have arrived. I ask your patience while preparations in the Courtroom are completed. I will return to gather you when all is ready."

His voice was weak and squeaky. He strained to make himself heard.

A number of hands flew up in the air with questions. But the Officer turned without further explanation, made his departure.

Silence resumed.

I picked up on the newspaper where I had left off. I tried to read through the page-one articles. As I read, my mind repeatedly wandered back to Dad. Back to his untimely and meaningless death. Back to my ambivalence. My eyes retraced the same printed lines over and over as I tried to focus on the news.

I couldn't recall the last time my own state of mind had troubled me to this degree. I tried to suppress my thoughts, only to have them rise again, constantly badgering me for answers.

Fortunately, I didn't need to struggle with the newspaper very long. It was only a few minutes before the Officer returned.

"All is ready," he said. "I will usher you into the Courtroom. There, you will each take a seat in the jury box. Your seat has been marked with your name. You will sit in your designated seat only.

"Please follow."

He turned and walked through the corner exit – presumably toward the Courtroom.

Jurors crowded toward the doorway, following the Officer. It was like Black Friday at Macy's, only in slow motion. No one pushed. The movement was more of a chaotic and clumsy budging.

Finally reaching the Courtroom proper, I continued forward, moving as one with the queue. As I shuffled along, I glanced around me.

This courtroom had been arranged differently from any other I had seen. There was no jury box near the front. There was no bar separating the trial participants from the gallery. In fact, there was no gallery. The jurors were taking their seats in the area where the spectators would usually sit – a space just large enough to accommodate chairs for all of us.

As the Jurors filed into their rows in the order in which they had followed the Officer, each found that their designated seat was positioned exactly where the queue had aligned them. I know I was more than a little surprised to find my name on a gold and black plastic placard on the back of the chair in the row precisely where my position in line came to a stop. Others were commenting to one another about the same coincidence.

No one appeared to be out of sequence. Everyone had arrived exactly at his or her assigned location.

Given the disordered and random formation of the queue, I wondered how the court had accomplished this feat of legerdemain. The Judge must have planned it out very carefully to produce a desired effect. I wondered what effect that might be.

Regardless of the Judge's intent – and by whatever means the seating chart had been arranged and accomplished – I was impressed with the ingenuity involved.

Taking my seat, and getting over the mild shock of the clever seating maneuver, I continued to inspect our venue.

Including the space where we sat, the room was maybe seventy feet long and fifty wide. There were no windows – only frames and lighting to simulate them.

The appearance of the Judge's Bench was within the bounds of normalcy. It was crafted of black walnut and dominated the front of the room.

The Counsel Tables were arranged strangely. Usually, counsel and clients sat at these tables with their backs to the gallery (where we now sat) and facing the Judge. The Counsel Tables in this room stood along the sides of the open floor space between the Jury and the Bench, facing one another. I supposed this made sense given the lack of a jury box and our viewpoint from the rear of the room. But it was highly unusual.

Between the Counsel Tables, a mostly empty rectangle about twenty feet in depth separated the 'Jury Box' from the Bench. In the center of this space, facing us, stood a simple wooden podium . . . a 'lectern' might be more accurate . . . probably the location from which the lawyers would address the Jury during *voir dire*.

Looking up, I noted that the Courtroom ceiling was arched, its surface painted to represent a blue sky with wispy clouds. Peaceful.

Once again, I began to feel at ease within the guardian walls of the court routine. This was a venue I understood – where I knew familiar rules would apply. My comfort in this place presented a stark contrast to the uneasiness I had experienced in the church a week earlier, more recently in my morning dreams, and again in the Assembly Room.

Then I noticed something unusual about the ceiling. The three-dimensional sky mural played optical tricks with exact estimates, but I guessed the ceiling arch to be about eighteen feet high at its peak. This courtroom must occupy parts of two stories in the court building – another anomaly, considering contemporary construction designs. At least I had never seen a multi-level courthouse with two-story courtrooms.

After seating us, the Court Officer had disappeared through a doorway in the left front corner of the Courtroom. The Judge's Chambers – his private office – would be back there.

The Officer now reappeared. First a man and then a woman followed. Each wore a dark suit and a white shirt – appropriate court attire for attorneys. The two lawyers took their places behind the Counsel Tables, but remained standing.

When Counsel were in position, the Court Officer called out as loudly as he could manage:

"All rise."

We stood.

"Hear ye! Hear ye! This Court is now in session. The Honorable Judge Jonathon Cole presiding."

All eyes turned to the Chambers doorway. As the Judge entered the Courtroom, he faded smoothly into focus from the darkness beyond. He was a bald man in a black robe, and had rolled through the doorway in a wheelchair.

The Judge had no legs – at least none were visible beneath his robe, and the chair showed no evidence of foot supports. On closer examination, the Judge was not only bald, but he also had no eyebrows, eyelashes or visible hair of any kind. His skin was pale to the point of translucence.

Possibly a sensitivity to sunlight?

Eschewing the modern convenience of a powered chair, the Judge used his arms and hands on the spoked wheels to roll himself up a ramp behind the Bench.

Outside the Jury's view, he transferred himself to the judicial high-back leather chair. Then he and the chair gradually rose until his bald head and robed shoulders eventually appeared above the Bench-top.

I couldn't help but pity the afflicted wretch. His must be an existence fraught with challenges, obstacles and prejudices. No doubt, he threw himself into his work as a respite from life's ever-present reminders of his oddity.

I observed the Judge as he surveyed the room. Despite first impressions, he possessed a judicial demeanor – one that demanded respect. I wondered by what life path he had traveled to enable him to overcome his physical limitations, and to develop that powerful presence.

His eyes passed over me. I felt their intensity.

"Be seated," the Court Officer squeaked.

The Jury pool and the lawyers all sat.

"Good morning," the Judge began, his voice calm, confident and strong. He faced the Jury. His head and body moved little as he spoke.

"Thank you for coming today.

"My first announcement may be a surprise to some of you who are familiar with typical jury selection procedures. But there will be no *voir dire* – no questioning of Jurors for today's trial."

The Judge seemed to be looking directly at me as he continued to speak.

"All of you have been chosen to serve as Jurors in this matter. There will be no further selection process. There will be no alternates. No one will be excused.

"To be perfectly clear . . . every one of you will serve."

So much for my day of contemplation and reflection. But what in the hell was this Judge thinking? Maybe he was a more pitiable specimen than I had first surmised. There were more than thirty of us prospective jurors here. The Judge's statement was absurd. The Court couldn't empanel more than twelve jurors, plus a couple alternates. The law didn't allow for it.

Before I had finished considering the Judge's bizarre statement, he interrupted my thoughts with another declaration . . . a statement I could never have anticipated . . . and words I will never forget.

"Today, you will determine if God exists."

Oh, for Pete's sake!

Some Jurors laughed. Some jeered. A few got up to leave. I looked for hidden video equipment. Had this Judge taken complete leave of his senses?

"Please be silent and sit down!"

The Judge's voice was not loud, harsh or irate. But it carried a weight of authority, requiring – no, demanding – compliance. At once, the room was silent. All Jurors retook their seats.

"I assure you, Ladies and Gentlemen of the Jury, this is no joke. In fact, this trial is most serious business ever undertaken by humankind."

I pinched my arm. *This had to be a dream.*

The Judge sat forward, perching leglessly on his chair.

"Ever since ancient humans began to think," he continued, "they have asked the same questions: 'Does God exist?' 'Is He . . . or She . . . out there somewhere?' 'Or are humans alone?'"

This deranged Judge was dead serious.

"Beginning this morning, and continuing as long as necessary, you thirty-six Jurors will weigh evidence offered by witnesses claiming expertise regarding God's existence . . . or the absence thereof.

"After you have heard all of the testimony, you will consider the evidence for and against the existence of God. And you will finally decide by your verdict, whether there is a God, or whether nature alone governs the universe."

This was ridiculous.

This whole affair was going to be a waste of my time. I should go back to the office and get some work done. I even started to get up from my seat. But something told me I shouldn't leave. I should play this farce out to its conclusion. Humor this demented Judge.

Although I could conceive of no rational reason why, I decided to stay.

CHAPTER 5
THE FIRST DELIBERATION

"The Court acknowledges the enormity of the issue you are asked to decide," the Judge went on.

His tone was calm . . . almost mundane . . . as if he were instructing just another Jury, in a just another trial.

"So the Court has made accommodations – in the form of physical changes to this Courtroom, procedural alterations to the typical trial rules, and other adjustments and modifications to the trial process – which will become apparent as the trial progresses.

"One such deviation from usual Courtroom protocol is that the Jurors will be excused from time to time to discuss the proceedings among themselves."

The Judge paused, again passing his gaze over each Juror in turn. His stare pierced my consciousness as it passed by.

"At this time, the Court will adjourn to allow Jurors to contemplate the task before them, and to prepare themselves to receive the evidence in whatever manner individual Jurors deem most suitable for their sensibilities."

'Suitable for their sensibilities?' What did he mean? Jurors receive evidence by paying attention, impartially, without bias. What 'sensibilities' could he be referring to?

The Judge nodded toward the Court Officer.

"All rise," the Officer said. Then, proceeding down the aisle toward the Assembly Room, he waved in our direction. "Follow me."

As we re-entered the Assembly Room, it was plain that the

seating here had changed. The steel chairs and large tables were gone. Dispersed throughout the room there were nine wooden tables, each with four wooden chairs – one chair on each side. The corners of the room had been segregated from the main area by fabric-covered office dividers, creating four booths, each about eight feet square.

Intrigued by the corner alcoves, I glanced into one of them and found a single wooden stool beside a smallish woven rug. A round, wooden lamp table occupied one side. On it stood a simple silver candlestick, holding an unlit, white taper. Stick matches and incense lay side-by-side on a silver tray.

After all the Jurors had returned to the Assembly Room, and were still milling about trying to decide where to sit, the Officer announced, "Locate the chair with your name on it. That chair, but not necessarily the table at which it is presently placed, will be your deliberation seat for the remainder of the trial. You may leave any belongings on your chair and they will be kept safe for you.

"The corner alcoves are available for occasional private contemplation. Please be mindful of others' needs and limit your time in the alcoves accordingly.

"Now . . . prepare yourselves to receive the evidence. I will return for you when it is time to proceed."

He did an about-face and exited through the Courtroom door.

The Officer's statements struck me as rote recitation. Not that such was unusual for court formalities. But in the context of this bizarre trial, his manner seemed oddly . . . comfortable?

By the time I found my chair, a woman was already seated at the table. She stood as I arrived.

I guessed her to be in her thirties. A brown head scarf covered most of her dark hair. The rest of her attire reminded me of the Somali refugee women who had settled in the Twin Cities area of late.

"Bill Kensey," I said, offering her my hand.

She did not accept my offer of a handshake, but smiled and bowed her head graciously.

"I am not allowed to return your hand greeting," she said, with a thick accent I couldn't identify. "But I accept it in the spirit it is offered. My name is Dariah. I wish you Allah's peace and prosperity."

"I accept your greeting with my thanks."

I duplicated her bow. We both remained standing – neither wanting to sit before the other. As we endeavored to resolve our seating priorities, another Juror approached our table.

Petite, with sandy-blond hair, she wore a tight-knit pink top over blue denim jeans. A surplus of perfume blossomed in the air around her. I was taken aback by her youthful appearance. She looked too young for a jury. Maybe sixteen?

Our new acquaintance cheerfully introduced herself as 'Ariel.'

Just then, our final table-mate arrived. The man was likely in his twenties, slim, oriental – probably Japanese – and wore a well-pressed, blue pinpoint cotton shirt and grey dress slacks. He nodded to each of us, but did not return our smiles. Once we had all taken our seats around the table, he told us his name was 'Tai.'

At first, we were silent, each taking in the chaos that swirled around us in the Assembly Room.

Everywhere we turned, Jurors were expressing reactions to the Judge's directives. At some tables, they were laughing and joking. Other Jurors stared blankly. Still others shouted angrily.

It seemed odd, but the acoustics in the room were such that, even though we were seated quite closely together, I couldn't make out a single word among those being exchanged at the other tables. An acoustical damper – or possibly a surplus of syllables uttered simultaneously – seemed to separate us from our fellow Jurors.

We would have to fend for ourselves regarding how to proceed.

At our table, no one had as yet spoken. I decided to get things started.

"So what do you make of the Judge's comments?" I asked, glancing at each of my table-mates in turn.

Tai was the first to respond.

"Total waste of our time. This is all foolishness. A trial to prove God?" A faint – but discernible – Japanese accent accompanied his words. The cadence of his speech was formal and crisp – as though English was not his native language.

He grunted, turning away from the table, crossing both arms and legs against anyone who might dissent.

"Do you think we're on TV?" Ariel asked, her bright eyes searching the room. "That would be so cool."

Her youthful exuberance was refreshing, though perhaps a bit inappropriate to the situation.

"Right now, I'm not certain what to think," I said. "I *am* certain, however, that this is not going to be any ordinary trial. I practice law, and nothing about the way things have been handled so far bears the slightest resemblance to any trial I've seen.

"Furthermore, this can't be a *real* trial – a trial of the law. How could anyone try the existence of God? Who would be the Plaintiff, and who the Defendant? How could any court obtain jurisdiction of this issue?

"No. Something else is going on here. Of that I am sure. A psychological experiment? Or a test of social interactions? I don't know. Something else."

Dariah spoke.

"Should we not take this matter seriously? What if it is we who are on trial? Should we not defend Allah?"

Tai scoffed and shook his head.

"You laugh at these proceedings," Dariah said to Tai. "Then please excuse yourself if you will not participate in good faith."

Tai said nothing. Instead, he examined his fingernails.

"Whatever may be happening right now," I said, "I suggest we remain civil with one another. This will be a long and unpleasant experience if we only antagonize and complain. Something unusual is going on in this courthouse. I for one am intrigued, though I can't explain why. I plan to go along with the charade and find out what.

"And Dariah, I can think of no reason you should not defend Allah, if that is your wish. In fact, I expect many Jurors will choose to defend or assert religious faith during this proceeding – and many others will denounce it."

I glanced around our table again.

"Are we agreed to give this circumstance a fair effort?"

"I like that idea," Ariel chimed in. "It's like an adventure. And maybe we'll be on TV after all."

"I like Ariel's spirit," I said. "Let's try to do what we're asked, and see where this leads us. The Judge said we should prepare ourselves to hear the evidence about God. How can we do that?

"Dariah. You are Muslim, correct?"

"Yes."

"And Ariel?"

"I'm not sure what I am. I go to church with my family every Sunday, though. And I know about Jesus."

"Tai. Will you humor us by participating?"

Tai uncoiled his defensive stance and turned back to the table with an exaggerated sigh. "Okay. You win."

He threw his hands in the air signaling defeat.

"Do you have a faith, Tai?"

"I have no faith in an all-powerful being. Is that what you're looking for from me?"

"I don't know what we're looking for, Tai," I said, with more patience in my tone than I truly felt. "I wish I did."

"For what it's worth, my background is Christian – Lutheran actually – though I'm not sure I can say I believe everything the Lutheran Church teaches. Some of the doctrine seems a bit . . . improbable."

Why had I said that? I've been Lutheran all my life. Was I ashamed to admit it?

There was another pause.

"So what now?" Ariel asked me.

I looked at Tai and Dariah. They seemed to expect an answer as well. I had somehow become the *de facto* moderator for my little group. This was turning into an interesting diversion. I no longer lamented the loss of my time for solitary contemplation.

"Prepare yourself to have an open mind about what you are going to see and hear in the Courtroom, I guess. That's what Jurors are supposed to do. Be prepared to hear the evidence. Then try to make your best decision on the issue. The Judge will probably give us more instructions. Follow those as well."

"So we get to decide if there is a God?" Ariel scrunched up her face and scratched the back of her head.

"So we are told," is all I could come up with.

"Look," I said, "this is the most bizarre situation I have ever encountered. I'm sure none of you has seen anything like it either. I suppose our choices are to go along, or to check out. I'm pretty sure there wouldn't be any legal repercussions if one or more of us chose to leave.

"There's the door," I said, mostly to Tai. "I think we're free to use it. But decide now. It may not be possible later."

I heard the words I had just spoken. What made me think they were true?

We sat in silence for a moment.

Dariah stood. "Please excuse me. I must pray."

She bowed toward us, then made her way between the tables to one of the corner alcoves.

"We get to tell God if He exists," Ariel said to no one in particular. "Cool!"

CHAPTER 6
OPENING ARGUMENTS

After half an hour of mostly chaos in the Jury Assembly Room, the Court Officer reappeared in the doorway.

"If I may have your attention, please."

Those who had not noticed his arrival now turned to listen.

"The Judge has called the Jury back to the proceedings. But before you return, he has ordered that you not bring any of the following articles into the Courtroom."

The Officer now read from a list on his clip board.

"No electronic devices such as cell phones, voice or video recorders, music players, radios or computers of any kind are allowed. Also prohibited are wristwatches, clocks and any other time-telling contrivances."

Contrivances? Interesting word choice.

Prohibition of electronics from the Courtroom was not uncommon. The judges didn't want jurors to be distracted. But watches?

"Please leave any forbidden articles, and other personal items of your choosing, on your seat. As I have said, we will see to their security during the trial, and your possessions will be returned to you afterward."

Jurors dug through their pockets, purses and briefcases, removing items to be left on their chairs and arranging them on the seats. Body postures and facial expressions indicated that there was a general reluctance to part with personal belongings. But there also appeared to be universal compliance. I left my watch, cell phone and newspaper on my seat.

When the jurors had emptied their pockets of prohibited items, the Court Officer asked for silence, then said, "Please follow me. Be seated only in the chairs designated with your name plates."

The assemblage lined up behind the Court Officer and we all made our way back into the empty Courtroom. Several of us attempted to divert down the rows of chairs where we knew we had sat previously. But the Court Officer guided us back into the queue. And we filed into the rows in the order of our positions in the line.

This time the line had placed me in a different row of seats than on my first visit to the courtroom. But when I arrived at the chair corresponding to my position in the queue, I checked the name plate on the seat back, and once again, my name appeared there.

There had been no obvious arranging of Jurors when the line formed in the Assembly Room. I wondered anew the means by which the Judge had arranged this result, for it could not be a coincidence. I took my seat and waited for those behind me to sit as well. A low murmuring indicated that others had also confronted the repeated seating anomaly. It was an extremely clever trick. I would try to learn the secret from court personnel after the trial was over.

At least I thought I would.

After seating the Jurors, the Officer moved back and forth among us, collecting watches, phones and contraband that some had evidently either neglected to leave behind in the Assembly Room, or had chosen to retain despite instructions to the contrary. He was very efficient and seemed to know exactly who possessed prohibited items, and who hadn't – skipping over many Jurors entirely.

Had we been under video surveillance?

When he had finished collecting devices and 'contrivances,' he placed them in a box and carried them through the Chambers doorway, advancing into the blackness and disappearing from our view.

When he reappeared a few moments later, he no longer held the box. The two lawyers followed behind the Officer and resumed standing positions behind the Counsel Tables.

The Court Officer announced: "All rise."

We stood.

"Hear ye! Hear ye! This Court is now in session. The Honorable Judge Jonathon Cole presiding."

It was hard not to laugh at a voice that reminded me of Mickey Mouse. But I maintained my composure.

The pale, hairless Judge again appeared from beyond the Chambers doorway in his wheel chair, rolled up the ramp without so much as a glance in our direction, and rose in the high-backed leather chair.

"Be seated," the Court Officer directed.

All sat.

"Ladies and gentlemen of the Jury, I am disheartened that I must begin with an admonishment. Many of you have already failed to follow my directions. When I gave you time to prepare to receive the evidence in this case, many of you did not take your obligations as Jurors seriously. You laughed at what you considered absurd. You refused to accept that which you did not understand, and therefore, made folly of it.

I realize that these responses are in your natures. So the Court will impose no sanctions at this time." The Judge leaned forward.

"But be warned. As I have already told you, this trial is a serious undertaking . . . and of utmost importance. Any further refusals to participate fully will be met with reprisals.

"Are we clear?"

No one spoke.

"I require an answer from each of you. Are we now clear regarding the ground rules for this proceeding? I will give instructions and you will follow them to the letter. Evidence will be presented before you. You will give it your complete attention and thoughtful consideration.

"Are we clear?"

A chorus of "Yes's," "Yes, Your Honors" and other indications of assent emanated from the Jury Box. Then all was silent.

"Cleton Danyon Thomas, stand up," the Judge ordered, his voice a mixture of sadness and frustration.

A tall, broad-shouldered man wearing a brown shirt and bolo tie stood up.

"You have not responded to my question. Are we clear concerning the ground rules for this trial?"

The man hooked his thumbs in his belt and tried to pull off a swagger. After a moment, he cleared his throat and said in a voice that wavered a bit, "Yessir. We are."

"Good. Please be seated, Mr. Thomas."

Mr. Thomas sat down.

"At this time," the Judge continued, "we will hear opening arguments of Counsel. The Jury is directed that statements by Counsel are not evidence. They are arguments, designed to persuade the Jury to view evidence in a particular light, or with a particular bias. Consider the arguments carefully, as they may assist you in your deliberations. But always remember, Counsel's statements are arguments, not evidence.

"Counsel for the Repudiation of God will speak first. Then Counsel for the Existence of God will offer her presentation.

"Are you ready, Counsel?"

The Judge looked at the man in the navy blue suit occupying the Counsel Table to our right.

He stood.

"Ready, Your Honor."

"Please proceed."

At once the lights in the Courtroom dimmed to near darkness. The Judge's Bench remained illuminated from a source I couldn't identify. The Judge himself was clearly visible, but the lighting surrounding both the Judge and the Bench was muted.

A brighter light encircled the male attorney as he moved to the lectern in the near center of the Courtroom. As with the Bench lighting, I was unable to locate the light's source. And no shadows were visible.

The remainder of the Courtroom lay steeped in blackness.

This Judge certainly had a flare for the dramatic. I couldn't help wondering if he had hidden a high voltage Tesla coil behind the Bench, and at the opportune moment, lightning would appear to spring forth from his hands. I had once witnessed a traveling fire-and-brimstone preacher who used that trick. Whenever parishioners' attention wandered, he would literally jolt them back with a stomp on the coil switch and a concurrent thrust of his arms toward the skies. The lightning from the coil, and its loud crack, would inevitably awaken any drifting minds and bring clarity of focus back to the pulpit.

Now that's the kind of stuff religion's famous for! But why did I find myself expecting to find it in a court of law?

Counsel was preparing to speak. As best I could, I ignored the theatrics and listened to his argument.

COUNSEL FOR THE REPUDIATION OF GOD:

"Ladies and gentlemen of the Jury."

The attorney was Anglo, with dark, wavy hair. His cheekbones protruded noticeably from a gaunt face. His voice was a confident baritone.

"For centuries philosophers, scientists, theologians, physicists, astronomers and common men and women from every walk of life have debated the question posed in this trial. 'Is there a God? Does God exist?'

"During the course of this Trial, you will hear Witnesses testify to their beliefs regarding the facts surrounding this question. Many of these Witnesses are experts in their fields of academic study. They know intimately the subjects of which they speak. In fact, they have greater knowledge in their areas of specialized expertise than I, or any of you, can ever hope to acquire by just by listening to them. Yet you are charged with deciding the absolute truth among their assertions – a formidable task.

"You will hear testimony from experts claiming to prove God's existence . . . and others claiming to prove the opposite. But their claims of 'God' or 'No God' are not evidence. They are conclusions. And conclusions are for you, the Jury, to draw.

"Listen carefully to the testimony for facts . . . for evidence . . . for signs of truthfulness or falsehood. But ignore the conclusions you will no doubt hear. You, and only you, are vested with the authority and the responsibility to reach conclusions . . . to find the truth. Does the evidence support a finding for, or against, the existence of God?

"Though some testimony may delve into areas of science, philosophy or theology with which you are unfamiliar, listen nevertheless for those statements that constitute evidence – assertions of fact.

"I suggest you apply the following approach to any testimony purporting to support the existence of God . . . to help you discern between facts and leaps of faith:

"If there is a God – all powerful and ever-present – would He not make His existence undeniably clear to you in this proceeding? Would such a Being leave room for any doubt that He is here among us? That He exists?

"When the scientists recite complex cosmological theories, and expound upon obscure and inaccessible veins of mathematical knowledge, if you are confused, ask yourself, 'Wouldn't God allow me to understand if He were here?'

"And when a theologian claims that God's presence is within all of us, and we have only to seek it, ask yourselves again: 'If God is all-loving, and cares for my so-called soul, would He not seek me out, instead of hiding Himself in obscurity?'

"As you hear each Witness speak, and you see the conviction they will, no doubt, bring to their testimonies, do not let yourselves be distracted by charismatic personalities, likeable voices, or handsome appearances. Listen closely to their words and ask: 'Is God obvious to me in their emphatic exhortations? Does He slap me in the face and say, 'I am here. Feel my hand'?'

"I will bring before you scholars, highly-regarded in their fields, and offer proof that God does not – and even *cannot* – exist. The words of these teachers are instructive. They appeal to reason, common sense, things you know from your own experiences to be true.

"But these Witnesses are not necessary to disprove God. For if He did exist, He would intervene in these proceedings, and in all aspects of life, and make it plain to us all . . . as plain as the person sitting next to you . . . that He *does* exist. His silence, His absence, His lack of intervention in any form, by themselves, will disprove His existence."

The speaker paused.

"Nevertheless, the trial will proceed, even though the verdict is a foregone conclusion.

"Yet, if somehow I am wrong . . . if God *is* here after all, and some insanity makes me oblivious to His presence . . . He will surely show Himself to you as you wait to pass judgment on His creation. If He does exist, you will surely know. There should be no doubt.

"If after hearing all the evidence, there remains a doubt in your mind . . . even the slightest uncertainty . . . how can God possibly be said to exist?"

The attorney again paused momentarily.

"In conclusion, I ask that you grant me this one concession. As you listen, think, learn, consider . . . ask yourselves again and again, 'Where is God in this trial? If I harbor any doubt concerning His existence . . . where is God?'

"Thank you in advance for your service."

Counsel for the Repudiation of God closed a folder of notes to which he had been infrequently referring, and returned to his table.

As he got farther from the lectern, the brightness of his light faded and the lighting intensity gradually increased on opposing counsel as she approached the podium.

By the time she arrived, the circle of light had reached full brightness, and Repudiation Counsel's Table had vanished. The Bench remained a golden glow behind the female attorney.

Counsel for the Existence of God was a slightly round black woman. She stood about five-foot-four with her hair worn short and curly. Her face was . . . 'pleasant' is probably the best word.

COUNSEL FOR THE EXISTENCE OF GOD:

"Ladies and Gentlemen of the Jury."

Like her lawyerly counterpart, her voice exuded confidence. Her smooth contralto contrasted with the man's deeper tone.

"In the past century alone, authors have penned literally hundreds of books either advocating or disputing God's existence. Many of you have seen or heard of recent books by atheists such as *The God Delusion* by Richard Dawkins, or *God is Not Great* by Christopher Hitchins. Or perhaps by Christians such as, *The Creator and the Cosmos* by Hugh Ross.

A show of hands please. Excluding study of your religion's holy texts, how many of you have read even one of those hundreds of books in its entirety?"

I looked around at the Jurors. They were all doing the same. Only one person held her hand in the air.

"Ms. Gentry," Counsel continued, speaking to the woman with her hand up, apparently having memorized her name, "in what context did you read such a book?"

Ms. Gentry stood.

"Comparative Religions class in college, Ma'am."

"Did this book change your beliefs about the existence or non-existence of God?"

"No. To be honest, I didn't really get it . . . the meaning of the book, that is."

"Thank you. Please be seated, Ms. Gentry."

The Juror sat down and our attention returned to the female Counsel.

"So if I understand correctly," she continued, "of the myriad writings concerning this issue of seemingly paramount importance –

the very existence of God – thirty-five of you have read none, and one of you has read one, which text she found to be inscrutable.

The attorney to a step to one side of the podium.

"Why would so many of us ignore writings, many by very learned scholars and extremely intelligent men and women, when the subject matter is of such ultimate impact on our lives?"

She scanned the Jurors, making sure all were paying attention.

"I believe the reasons we avoid these books are twofold. One reason, Ms. Gentry has already articulated. We believe the discussion of God in these books will be 'too deep' or 'too academic' for us to comprehend, and will, therefore, be of no use to us – or may even confuse us.

"In many cases, this reason is valid. Some authors seem to revel in the complexity of their thought processes. The fewer people who can follow their thinking with clarity, the fewer who can claim to compare with the author's own intellect and expertise. These books are written more to increase the author's prestige among his or her peers, than to truly answer the question of God's existence for the masses.

"The second reason I believe the average person fails to read these texts is that, for the most part, people are comfortable with their own pre-established beliefs regarding God . . . or the absence of God.

"We are Muslim, Buddhist, Christian, Jew, Hindu, Atheist, Agnostic, or whatever other label we have selected for ourselves. We are comfortable with our chosen viewpoint, and uncomfortable with any idea that might pop our theistic or atheistic bubble. So we avoid controversial 'proofs' of 'God' or 'No God,' choosing to remain blissfully unaware of any challenges such writings may pose to our beliefs.

"In other words, we're happy with our current religious status – 'thank you very much.'

"Whatever your personal reason for not actively confronting the issue of God's existence before now, you had best suspend it for the duration of this trial. You are face-to-face with every human's decision of a lifetime. And you will have no choice but to render a verdict – 'God' or 'No God.' Pure natural forces, or divine interference. Randomness, or some higher purpose.

"These are weighty questions, to be sure. But they are yours to resolve, nonetheless.

"As you hear the evidence, I ask that you approach this decision with an open mind. Ask of yourselves all questions you think are relevant – not only the questions opposing Counsel proposes.

"If your mind remains shut, and during this trial God should slap you in the face, I daresay that you will write it off as a twitch in your nervous system. If you continue to hide behind indelible decisions you have already made, when God appears before your eyes, your mind will cast His revelation as deception or trickery.

"I offer this warning. Do not underestimate your ability to deceive yourself. Open your thoughts and your minds to see God and you *will* see Him. Shut the door in His face, and you cannot.

"You are about to hear evidence that will befuddle you, that will outdistance your ability to comprehend, and that will challenge every belief and understanding you have ever held about the existence of God. You have within you the ability to decide. You are made in His image. And though your eyes may not see, you will recognize Him. Though your ears may not hear, you will perceive His voice. Though his Spirit passes through you without arousing a single human sensation, you will know His presence.

"Here . . . in this Courtroom . . . I promise you, *you will meet God.*

"Will you vindicate Him? Or deny what you know to be true? Your verdict will be your answer.

"Thank you for your service. And may God's Spirit be upon you all."

The female attorney had not referred to any notes that I could tell. At least she took none from the lectern back to her table. The light on her, as she walked away from the podium, faded to darkness.

The only illumination remaining in the room was the constant glow surrounding the Judge and his Bench.

CHAPTER 7
THE ANTHROPOLOGIST

The Judge turned in the direction where we had last seen the male attorney.

JUDGE: "Counsel. Are you prepared to call your first Witness?"

The circle of light appeared around the attorney. He was already standing.

COUNSEL: "I am, Your Honor."

JUDGE: "Please proceed."

I looked around to locate the door through which the Witness would appear. When I didn't see the Witness enter, I turned back to the Bench, and the Witness Stand beside it. The Witness was already seated in the stand.

I turned and whispered to a Juror next to me. "Did you see where she came from?"

"I'm afraid I didn't see," she whispered. "I was watching one door, as she must have come through another."

I returned my attention to the front of the Courtroom. Two bright circles of light now enveloped the attorney and the Witness. The Judge and Bench continued their softer glow. All else remained impenetrably dark. Even when I squinted, I couldn't make out the slightest hint of the Court Officer or the opposing Counsel.

The male attorney approached the Witness, stopping about ten feet away and to the right of her. The lawyer's positioning was classic. The angle of his body allowed him to direct his questions to the Witness, while the Jurors could still see and hear the questioning clearly.

The Witness was a middle-aged white woman with brown hair. Beneath an olive suit, her white collar was buttoned up tight.

The attorney asked the Witness to identify herself. A Juror behind me coughed at the instant the Witness told us her name. So I didn't hear it. I *did* hear her credentials, though. She was a doctor of anthropology at a research institute, and her list of honors and publications was extensive.

COUNSEL FOR REPUDIATION: "Doctor. Could you describe for us your religious affiliations, if any?"

WITNESS: "Personally, I see no evidence that there is a God, and therefore, I do not ascribe to the notion that one exists."

Her manner of speech was formal and smacked of a lecture hall.

COUNSEL: "In your opinion, Doctor, does science have anything to say about the existence of God?"

WITNESS: "I don't believe science and God are necessarily connected at all. But there are certainly many Christians and Jews who would disagree with me."

COUNSEL: "Please elaborate."

WITNESS: "Darwin's Theory of Evolution has seemed to be most troubling to Jews and Christians because the evolution of man – and for that matter, the universe – does not correlate with creation stories relayed in the Bible. Although I am not a theologian, I believe the crux of the issue lies in the Biblical accounts of creation occurring over a period of six days, and God creating man from dust, sometime between four and ten thousand years ago."

COUNSEL: "How does science, and evolution in particular, contradict these Biblical accounts?"

WITNESS: "Let's start with the time-frame for creation of the universe. It is very widely accepted among scientists that the universe had its beginning no less than 13.7 billion years ago. In fact, astronomers have located, viewed and positively identified galaxies that are more than 12 billion years old. So to a scientist, the very idea that the universe may be only several thousand years old is ludicrous.

"Beyond the astronomical observations, work here on Earth has confirmed that our own planet is demonstrably more than 3.9 billion years old. The ages of numerous rock specimens have been determined, and confirmed by multiple methods, to exceed that age. It is also known that the earth's surface was molten for hundreds of millions of years before any solid rocks could have formed.

"So again, the idea of a universe, or even an earth, that is only a few thousand years old is as close to impossible as can be proven by any objective measure."

COUNSEL: "So I understand you to say that the universe and the earth are much older than the Bible indicates."

WITNESS: "Not only much older . . . older by many orders of magnitude."

COUNSEL: "What about the age of the human species? Does science have *evidence* of how long humans have lived on earth?"

He looked pointedly at the Jury as he spoke the word 'evidence.'

WITNESS: "Anthropological studies, aided by work in archaeology, genetics and other scientific disciplines, have proven that humans, in one form or another, have walked the earth for millions of years. Anthropologists and archaeologists continue to unearth more and more human fossils on a regular basis.

"The oldest fossil evidence of upright-walking humans was discovered in October of 2009. The skeletal species dubbed *Ardipithecus ramidus*, and nicknamed 'Ardi,' is an ancestor of modern humans who lived in Africa about 4.2 million years ago.

"*Homo sapiens*, or modern man, has existed for at least two hundred thousand years. Numerous skeletal remains confirm this fact. From an evidentiary standpoint, there is no doubt that humans have been around far longer than any traditional or literal interpretation of Biblical timetables allows.

"Besides the history of humanity, the idea of humans being 'created' from dust is entirely contrary to the laws of evolution.

"If we pare the term 'evolution' down to its purest form, the Theory of Evolution states simply that every species had a living parent species. Contrary to popular thinking, Darwin's further theorizing that natural selection caused the survival of one species over another is *not* central to evolutionary science.

"If we examine ancient rock strata around the world, the evidence of evolution is irrefutable. In the oldest layers of rock, there are no fossil remnants at all – therefore no life existed during this time. In slightly more recent layers, evidence of extremely elementary organisms appears. Moving higher in the rock strata, and forward in time, we observe increasingly complex life forms.

Single cell organisms give way to multi-celled plants such as algae. It is only within the last 600 million years that increasingly complex species . . . worms, fish, land plants, insects, reptiles, amphibians, birds, then finally mammals . . . begin to appear. In each case, we see the developments that occurred in the parent species which led to its successor.

"Following this extremely well-documented progression from very, very simple organisms, without even a means of locomotion, to modern humans, with their advanced cognitive and adaptive abilities, it is only possible to conclude that the complex species we now call 'man' has evolved through many evolutionary 'parents' to reach its current state of functionality.

"Humans most certainly were *not* created from inanimate dust. Nor could they have evolved over less than billions of years.

"To summarize, the Bible is demonstrably inaccurate in at least these three assertions:

"One – God created the universe over a six-day period.

"Two – The universe and the earth are only about four to ten thousand years old.

"Three – God made man from dust and created him in a single day.

"Mainly for these reasons, many Christians and Jews deny the fact of evolution, clinging instead to scientifically unsupportable beliefs."

COUNSEL: "I'm sure some Jurors are wondering, so I'm going to ask this question. Does science explain how the very first life appeared on earth, apparently without a living parent species?"

WITNESS: "Some scientists theorize that, in the 'primordial stew' of warm ancient oceans, increasingly complex inanimate molecules, such as amino acids and proteins, may have spontaneously combined to form the first living creature's DNA – its blueprint for existence. This theory has yet to be proven to my satisfaction.

"In my opinion, science does not have sufficient evidence to offer an explanation for the origin of life on earth at this time. Without evidence, this is not a question that a competent scientist should attempt to answer on the witness stand. Theologians and philosophers speculate regarding such matters. True scientists do not."

COUNSEL: "Thank you, Doctor. You have been very helpful."

Then turning to the Judge, Counsel said, "I have no further questions for this Witness."

Counsel for Repudiation picked up his notes and yielded the floor to his female counterpart.

The female attorney assumed a stance resembling that of the male counsel, but angling in the opposite direction, and standing to the left of the Witness. She stood with hands folded just below her waist.

JUDGE: "Please proceed with your cross, Counsel."

COUNSEL FOR EXISTENCE: "Thank you, Your Honor." Then turning to the Witness, "Doctor. Does science have anything to say about the question of when modern humans became self-aware?"

The Witness paused a moment in thought.

WITNESS: "Could you define that term as used in your question, please?"

COUNSEL: "Certainly. I define 'self-awareness' as the knowledge of oneself as an individual, together with the ability to make rational decisions involving the individual's self-interest."

WITNESS: "Scientists are able to determine if a living person is conscious or unconscious, if she responds to stimuli, like a poke or a bright light, or if her nervous system is functioning within normal parameters. I am not aware that science delves into the history of self-awareness. Furthermore, I'm not sure how self-awareness could be scientifically proven to exist at a given time in history."

COUNSEL: "So if I understand you correctly, when you speak of human evolution, you are expressing no professional opinion about when humans became self-aware."

WITNESS: "No. That is correct."

COUNSEL: "Or when – or even *if* – humans became possessed of a soul."

WITNESS: "No. These are not anthropological or scientific issues."

COUNSEL: "Just so we are perfectly clear . . . you have no way to *disprove* that God may have given man a soul about four to six thousand years ago, and before that, *homo sapiens* was just another animal."

WITNESS: "No. But I am also not aware of any scientific evidence that modern humans are *not* just another animal – albeit a highly functioning one – or that humans do, in fact, possess a soul."

COUNSEL: "Let's pose a hypothetical situation for you to consider. Please assume that God created the entire universe in six, twenty-four-hour days."

I could see the Witness roll her eyes.

COUNSEL: "Please bear with me, Doctor. Take my assumption as true."

WITNESS: "Very well."

COUNSEL: "Couldn't an all-powerful God create all of the evidence, just as astronomers, archaeologists, anthropologists and other scientists have found it, and made that evidence appear to indicate a much older universe? Or an evolutionary history for man?

"Couldn't an omnipotent God fool scientists into thinking the cosmos, the earth, humans, are much older than they actually are?"

WITNESS: "It's a silly question. Even if God does exist, why would God do such a thing?"

COUNSEL: "I do not ask for an interpretation of God's motives, Doctor . . . only whether my hypothesis could be true."

The Witness paused for a moment.

WITNESS: "I am not qualified to answer that question. It is beyond my field of expertise."

COUNSEL: "I see. Thank you, Doctor." Then to the Judge, "No more questions, Your Honor."

As Counsel for Existence returned to the darkness of her table, Counsel for Repudiation rose. A spotlight illuminated him, as if on cue.

COUNSEL FOR REPUDIATION: "Redirect, your Honor?"

JUDGE: "Please proceed. But limit your redirect to issues raised on cross-examination. We have far to go in these proceedings."

COUNSEL: "Thank you, Your Honor."

The male attorney assumed his forty-five-degree stance between Witness and Jury.

COUNSEL: "Doctor. I also have a hypothetical for you."

WITNESS: "Very well."

COUNSEL: "Please assume for purposes of this question that I have a fairy in my pocket."

The Witness chuckled. And many Jurors did as well.

COUNSEL: "This fairy is all-powerful, but is entirely invisible and undetectable by any sensory or scientific means. Doctor, do you understand the assumptions I have outlined?"

WITNESS: "I believe I do."

COUNSEL: "Keeping in mind her assumed omnipotence, can you scientifically prove to me that my fairy is *not* responsible for creating the universe?"

WITNESS: "I don't suppose I could."

Counsel turned directly toward the Jury as he asked the Witness his next question.

COUNSEL: "In your experience as a highly-educated scientist, do you have an opinion as to whether a ridiculous assumption may lead to absurd conclusions?"

WITNESS: "Yes. Frequently."

Counsel turned back to face the Witness.

COUNSEL: "Thank you, Doctor." Then to the Judge, "No further questions."

JUDGE: "The Witness is excused."

CHAPTER 8
THE PHILOSOPHER

I wondered what time it was. It seemed like we should be breaking for lunch soon. Of course, no one had a watch. And there wasn't a clock to be found in the Courtroom itself. I knew this was by design. But the whole idea of placing the Jurors in a dark void without a clock – separating them, in a sense, from both space and time – was undeniably extreme.

I watched the Judge as the male attorney prepared to call his next Witness. The Judge sat with his arms bent at nearly ninety degree angles, forearms resting on the top of the Bench. He appeared comfortable in the leather chair, waiting patiently for the proceedings to continue.

The second Witness appeared out of the darkness of the Witness Stand when it was re-illuminated. I assumed that the first Witness had escaped my detection in a similar manner. At the time, it seemed likely that there had to be a hidden doorway either under, or behind, the Witness Stand. In the darkness, it was impossible to say.

The man in the Witness Chair appeared to be in his sixties or seventies. He was slender, with a shock of bright white hair. He wore a grey sport coat and a light-grey, button-down oxford shirt open at the neck. His small, black Poindexter glasses magnified his eyes distractingly.

REPUDIATION COUNSEL: "Please state your name for the Court."

WITNESS: "My name is Professor [indistinguishable]."

The Witness told us his name, but a noise (in this case, a creaking chair) prevented my hearing it. No matter. His name was not important, only his credentials and credibility.

REPUDIATION COUNSEL: "And what are your qualifications to testify at this proceeding, Professor?"

WITNESS: "I hold doctoral degrees in philosophy and sociology. I have written extensively for professional journals. And I have taught college and postgraduate courses in philosophy – particularly philosophy of religion – for several decades."

It was an impressive-sounding background, though perhaps a bit insulated from the world outside academia.

I suddenly realized that I was becoming invested in this proceeding, however ludicrous its premise, and I actually looked forward to hearing the evidence this Witness had to offer. *Perhaps this fake trial was the perfect remedy for my distraction over the religious ambiguity that had seemed to haunt me of late.*

COUNSEL: "Professor. How do you characterize your views and beliefs regarding God? Can you place yourself in a category with which the Jury might identify?"

The professor smiled and eased back in his chair. He folded his hands, pressing his index fingers together at his chin. He held this pose momentarily before speaking.

WITNESS: "While I prefer to consider myself an independent thinker, I suppose most people would consider me an atheist. To clarify, I do not believe there is a God. I do not, however, believe in forcing my views upon others. If a person is determined that God exists, I have no need to convince them otherwise.

"But logic and reason, the two sacred tools of the philosopher, argue strongly against the existence of any all-powerful or transcendent being."

The Professor's tone was conversational . . . just a neighbor visiting over the fence.

COUNSEL: "Professor. As a philosopher, is it common for you to construct proofs of logical arguments?"

WITNESS: "Yes. Often."

COUNSEL: "This trial today is an argument of sorts . . . an argument over the issue of God's existence. So Professor, if I asked you to prove to me whether God, or a Godlike Being, existed, where would you start?"

WITNESS: "In any deductive reasoning process, one must begin with a proper set of definitions. If terms, like 'God,' are ill-defined, logic can lead us to many conflicting conclusions."

COUNSEL: "And how would you define 'God' – for purposes of this trial, that is?"

WITNESS: "I would define that term in the context in which I believe most people use it. In the eyes of those who believe in a 'God,' most would agree that such a Being has certain attributes that qualify it as a 'God.'

"For example, God is all-powerful . . . or some would use the term, omnipotent. Both words have the same meaning. Most believers would also say that God is all-knowing – or omniscient – and that God is supremely loving toward humanity. God is present everywhere – or omnipresent. He is not bound by the laws of nature. So He 'transcends' our physical universe.

"One final characteristic of God has to do with His supposed relationship to humankind. It is widely believed that God has given humans 'free will' – at least within certain boundaries. In other words, God does not pull a puppet string for every human decision. So the God in my proofs will allow humans to have at least some free will to make their own decisions.

"Therefore, if I began to postulate a proof of God's existence, I would start with those terms as defining what I mean by the word 'God.' Omnipotent. Omniscient. All-loving. Omnipresent. Transcendent. And allowing humans a measure of free will."

COUNSEL: "Please offer us an example of one such 'proof,' if you wouldn't mind."

WITNESS: "Certainly.

"Because of God's purported transcendent characteristics, it is difficult to point to specific evidence of God within our universe. He 'transcends' space and time as we know them. We cannot detect Him by scientific means. So the logical approach is to determine if we can *disprove* God's existence. In other words, we would show that God *cannot* exist because His characteristics are impossible, irrational or inconsistent with what we know to be true.:

COUNSEL: "Interesting approach, Professor."

WITNESS: "Thank you.

"Here is one example:

"If God is all-powerful, He can do anything, including making an object that will never move, regardless of the forces applied in an attempt to move it. But God can also make a force so powerful that no object can resist it. The coexistence of an immovable object and an irresistible force is not rationally possible. Therefore, an omnipotent God cannot exist."

Counsel turned toward the Jury.

COUNSEL: "Please enlighten us with further examples, if you are able."

WITNESS: "They are endless. Here is another:

"If God is omniscient, he knows every decision that every human will ever make, even before the human makes that decision. But if God knows in advance every decision humans will make, then humans have no ability to make decisions differing from those God has foreseen. In other words, humans do not have the free will to alter such decisions. So if humans have any free will at all, God cannot be omniscient. Free will of humans is inconsistent with the omniscience of God."

COUNSEL: "I see."

WITNESS: "Here is another scenario for you to consider.

"If God is all-powerful, all-knowing and supremely loving toward humans, then He would have the power and the knowledge to show His love in an absolute and incontrovertible way. Yet in the real world, we see human suffering at every turn. Millions of children starving every year. Thousands drowned in tsunamis. Entire civilizations blotted out by volcanic eruptions. Untold suffering by torture and human conflict. If God knew all of these horrors would occur – because He is omniscient – and He had the power to prevent them – because He is omnipotent – and He did not do so, how can He be said to be supremely loving?

"I could give many more instances of contradictions, inconsistencies and illogical results that would result from God's purported existence if you wish?"

COUNSEL: "Thank you for your offer, Professor. But the Jury will have much evidence to consider. And I believe you have stated your approach concisely."

WITNESS: "My pleasure."

COUNSEL: "I have no further questions for this Witness, Your Honor."

Counsel for the Repudiation of God returned to his table and, again on cue, his light went dark.

The Judge turned toward opposing Counsel.

"Do you wish to cross examine the Witness?"

COUNSEL FOR EXISTENCE: "Yes. Thank you, Your Honor."

The woman attorney assumed her questioning position in the bright circle.

COUNSEL FOR EXISTENCE: "Professor. You would consider yourself an intelligent person, would you not?"

WITNESS: "Yes, I suppose I would."

COUNSEL: "And I believe you said that reason and logic are the 'sacred tools' of the philosopher. Am I remembering correctly?"

WITNESS: "Yes. And that is what I believe to be true."

COUNSEL: "Given your vast experience in philosophy – the use of logic and reason to resolve questions of the mind – would you agree that your greatest intellectual strengths lie in the areas of logic and reason, as opposed to, say, organizational behavior or medicine?"

The Witness puzzled over this question momentarily.

WITNESS: "I would have to agree with that statement. Yes."

COUNSEL: "But you must also agree that logic and reason do not provide humankind with complete answers to every problem confronting human existence. I mean, you wouldn't presume to use logic or reason to cure someone with a brain tumor. You would leave that concern to a brain surgeon. Correct?"

WITNESS: "Of course. It would be preposterous for me to 'reason' a tumor from a person's skull."

COUNSEL: "Precisely. And you wouldn't expect a brain surgeon to match your knowledge and abilities when it comes to philosophical matters. Would you?"

WITNESS: "Of course, a brain surgeon could also be a philosopher. But normally, I would not expect a surgeon to possess extensive knowledge of philosophy."

COUNSEL: "Nor a biologist."

WITNESS: "No. Not ordinarily."

COUNSEL: "Nor a rocket scientist, nor a chemist, nor even the President of the United States."

WITNESS: "Extensive knowledge of the methods of philosophical reasoning would not typically be required in such occupations. No."

COUNSEL: "Persons working in each of the specialties I have mentioned almost certainly would know more than you do about their respective occupations. Isn't that true?"

WITNESS: "I should hope so. But I fail to see how any of this is relevant to my proofs."

COUNSEL: "My point, Professor, is that every discipline has experts who wield the 'sacred tools' of that discipline with indisputable expertise. Yet you believe that *your* 'sacred tools' – reason and logic – are the appropriate ones for disproving God.

"Among all professions and areas of academic inquiry, and all the various methods used to achieve proficiency in such pursuits, what causes you to believe that philosophers hold the requisite knowledge to disprove God?"

WITNESS: "My dear woman. I understand that you are defending your side of this argument. But logic and reason are the supreme tools for understanding abstractions such as have been posed to me today. They are the highest order of human thought. Everyone knows that something has to at least make sense in order for it to exist. I can't claim to possess superhuman strength and expect anyone to believe such a statement. It is nonsense. That is, it is unreasonable. It is not logical.

"Reason and logic are the first tests any theory must pass. They alone may not provide enough evidence to prove every valid hypothesis to be true. Other expertise, such as scientific studies, may be required. But they most certainly suffice to prove many propositions false.

"To deny this fact is both unreasonable and nonsensical."

COUNSEL: "If I understand what you are saying, Professor, in order for any proposition to be true, it must first survive the application of reason and logic."

WITNESS: "Yes."

COUNSEL: "Those are the 'sacred tools' by which every proposition must be measured."

WITNESS: "Yes."

COUNSEL: "Professor. I mean no disrespect to you or your very impressive credentials. But what if your 'sacred tools' turn out to be dull?"

The Witness looked confused.

WITNESS: "I don't follow."

COUNSEL: "Could a brain surgeon be expected to achieve positive surgical results using only a chain saw and a screwdriver? Or an astronomer see the stars clearly through a scratched telescope lens?

"Professor . . . what if logic and reason are not the precision instruments you assume them to be? That many people assume them to be. What if they are faulty in some significant way? How would we know of their deficits? How would we prove they lead to invalid conclusions?"

The Professor thought for quite a while before answering.

WITNESS: "I can think of no way to make such a proof.

"However, I must say in the defense of logic and reason, that they have served mankind well, in many ways, for millennia. And to discount their importance or conclusions would be roughly equivalent to throwing out the laws of physics."

COUNSEL: "Please don't misunderstand, Professor. I do not advocate to throw them out – only to have their blades sharpened to a precision where they can help us make 'reasonable' decisions about God. At present, when it comes to God, reason and logic are the brain surgeon's metaphorical chainsaw. The tools are simply not up to the task."

WITNESS: "I'm afraid you and I will have to disagree on that point, Counsel."

COUNSEL: "Perhaps not. Maybe we can find an example where we agree that reason and logic are inadequate. Let's try this one.

"Can you prove, using only reason and logic, that I exist?"

WITNESS: "Certainly. There is a great deal of objective evidence of your existence. I can see you. I can hear you. If you were close enough to me, I could touch your arm. Since I can see, hear and touch you, you must therefore exist."

COUNSEL: "Sight, hearing, touch – these are all sensations of which you are aware because your brain has processed them for you. Correct?"

WITNESS: "I suppose."

COUNSEL: "Do you ever have dreams, Professor?"

WITNESS: "Yes."

COUNSEL: "And in your dreams, do you ever experience the sensations of seeing, hearing or touching people or things?"

WITNESS: "Yes."

COUNSEL: "Then according to your reasoning, the people and objects in your dreams must exist. Correct?"

WITNESS: "They exist in my subconscious mind – not in reality."

COUNSEL: "In that case, please allow me to rephrase my question. Since you have indicated that the sensations of sight, hearing and touch prove my existence 'in reality,' the people and objects you sense in your dreams must also exist 'in reality.' Correct?"

The Witness shifted in his chair.

WITNESS: "Perhaps my proof was not correctly constructed. I did have to prepare it on short notice. Please allow me another attempt."

COUNSEL: "By all means."

WITNESS: "I could ask others to confirm that you exist. They could perform any tests they deemed necessary to confirm your existence. Then their conclusions would be combined with mine to show that you exist in reality, and not just in my mind."

COUNSEL: "And who would confirm the existence of the 'others' to whom you refer?"

The Witness was visibly frustrated. He made an attempt to maintain the appearance of objectivity.

WITNESS: "You are saying that my second proof raises the same questions as my first. Regardless of how many witnesses I may bring forth in support of your existence, proving *their* existence is just as problematic as proving yours . . . or for that matter . . . proving mine.

"But the flaw in your approach, Counsel, is that each of us *knows* of our existence, and of the existence of those around us. It is self-evident. Life has no meaning without such knowledge. Assuming the opposite – that none of us really exists – leads to worthless conclusions.

"You may have heard that a fellow named Descartes resolved the logical problem of one's own existence hundreds of years ago when he declared, 'I think; therefore, I am.'"

The philosopher was sounding quite impressed with himself, and spoke to the attorney as if to a child.

COUNSEL: "No disrespect meant to Descartes, Professor, but his conclusion was not based on reason or logic. It was based on his personal *belief* that his existence was self-evident. Correct?"

The Witness shifted again in his chair.

WITNESS: "I suppose that is true."

COUNSEL: "And Descartes never was able to *logically prove* the existence of himself, or of anyone else in the world, was he?"

WITNESS: "I would have to concede that he was not able to do so."

COUNSEL: "So logic and reason cannot even prove that *you* exist or that *I* exist, and you still maintain that your 'sacred tools' are not just a tiny bit too dull to disprove *God's* existence?"

She held her thumb and forefinger close together before her eyes, illustrating the small degree of dullness necessary to confirm her argument.

WITNESS: "Not at all. Your question presents a false analogy. I challenge you to pose another."

COUNSEL: "I admire the tenacity with which you cling to your conclusions, Professor . . . despite all logic and reason to the contrary.

"Thank you for your time." Then to the Judge, "No further questions for this Witness."

Counsel for Existence returned to her table as her light faded away.

Counsel for Repudiation rose. The lighting made its usual adjustments, falling on Repudiation Counsel as he said, "Redirect, Your Honor?"

This time he remained at his table as he questioned the philosopher.

COUNSEL: "Professor. In your extensive studies, teachings and writings, and in your vast experience using reason and logic to resolve all manner of questions of human interaction, have you ever had cause to believe that either reason or logic can, by any stretch of the imagination, be considered inaccurate or defective?"

WITNESS: "Never."

COUNSEL: "No further questions for this Witness, Your Honor."

JUDGE: "Professor, you are excused."

The lighting around the Witness Stand and Counsel, once again, faded to blackness. A bright light now encircled the Judge. The translucence of his skin in the whiteness was startling.

The Judge leaned forward and focused intently on the Jurors.

Though there was no way I could possibly tell at this distance, I again felt as though he was looking particularly at me. He paused. I felt his penetrating stare once more. Then he leaned back to his normal seated position and gave the Jurors their instructions.

JUDGE: "At this time, I am going to excuse the Jury from the Courtroom to allow you to consider and discuss the evidence presented up to this point.

"I caution you not to draw final conclusions regarding the subject matter of this trial until you have heard all of the evidence. But it would be asking too much of the human mind to consider all arguments simultaneously. Deliberate and meditate on what you have heard so far. Then I will call you back to the Courtroom to receive further evidence."

Excusing the Jury for *partial* deliberations was unprecedented. Jurors were always instructed to wait for all the evidence to be offered before discussions between them should begin. But by this time, nothing about this trial, or this Judge, was going to surprise me.

I arose with the crowd as the lighting level increased to normal intensity across the entire room. Counsel remained standing behind their respective tables as the Court Officer led us out.

CHAPTER 9
THE SECOND DELIBERATION

When we returned to the Assembly Room, it came as no particular surprise to me that the seating had, once again, been rearranged. The same four-person tables were there. But my designated chair was not at the table where I had previously sat.

As I crossed the room, I noted that many chairs held purses, jackets, briefcases and other personal items the Jurors had left behind on their previous visit here. But I didn't see any watches, radios, cell phones or any of the items the Judge had designated contraband in the Courtroom itself. I worked my way methodically around the floor, looking for my gold and black name plate on a chair back, and finally locating it in the far left corner of the room.

I was the first to arrive at my table. As I expected, my watch and cell phone were nowhere to be found. The newspaper was there, though. I noted from the other name plates that among my table-mates was Tai, the combative oriental with whom I had sat during the last deliberation.

The next juror to find her seat at my table was an American Indian woman. In her early to mid-twenties, she wore her long, straight hair parted in the middle and tucked behind her ears. Her shirt was a button-front Native American design on chambray. A colorful beaded necklace adorned her neck.

I stood to welcome her.

She told me her name was Kimi. She pronounced it 'Kee-Mee.'

"That's a pretty name," I said, as she sat down across the table from me.

I sat as well.

"Thank you," she replied softly.

Kimi posed primly on the hard wooden chair, resting her deep-brown eyes on the delicate hands in front of her.

"Kimi," I said, waiting for her to make eye contact before proceeding.

"I haven't heard the name 'Kimi' before. Does it have a special meaning?"

She paused for a moment before answering.

"Kimi means 'secret' in the tongue of my ancestors."

There were a few seconds of awkward silence. Then Kimi asked, "What might your name be, sir?"

"William. But I'm afraid its meaning isn't nearly as mysterious or beautiful as yours. It means 'helmet' in Old German. But I'm not German at all – mostly of English descent, actually. In English, as you know, 'will' means 'determination' or 'desire.' I'd prefer to be thought of as 'determined,' rather than 'helmeted,' if you don't mind."

Kimi laughed. A shy smile showed briefly on her face, and then was gone.

"Actually, most people call me Bill. I'd appreciate it if you would do the same."

"Then I will call you 'Mr. Bill,' since it is my tradition to honor my elders in this manner."

"If you insist on the 'Mister,' then perhaps we should go with 'Mr. William.' 'Mr. Bill' has some connotations from a series of 'Saturday Night Live' skits I would rather avoid."

I smiled.

"Yes. Of course, Mr. William."

She returned the smile.

Another juror approached our table. I recognized Mr. Thomas as the rule-breaker who had drawn the Judge's attention during our last Courtroom session.

"Bill Kensey," I said, standing and offering him a handshake.

He stood at least six-foot-three. His brown plaid shirt and gold-tipped, bolo tie struck me as unusual for a Minnesotan. A transplanted Texan, perhaps?

He reached out his large, well-calloused hand and shook mine with vigor.

"The name's Cleton Danyon Thomas. But ya'll can call me Clete," he said, speaking to both of us. His confidence showed no ill effects of the Judge's admonition.

Tai arrived presently. After a further exchange of greetings and an introduction of Tai to the other two Jurors, I resolved to sit quietly for a while and listen to what my co-deliberators had to say.

Kimi's posture was perfect, and her breathing calm, as she posed serenely, her fingers now interlaced in her lap. Tai's hands fidgeted as he squirmed in his chair. Clete, who I had expected would start things off with some blustering, or perhaps a statement of brazen obnoxiousness, sat with arms folded across his chest. Clete's posture suggested that he was ready to challenge any opinion someone else at the table might be brave enough to share.

Ultimately, it was Tai who spoke first.

"I think the man's opening statement made sense. If there were a God, wouldn't He make himself obvious to us? The more I understand, and the more we as people understand, about the world through science, the less need we need to turn to superstition and so-called miracles for explanations. We don't burn witches anymore, do we.

"Of course, there are phenomena that we don't *yet* comprehend and can't *yet* fully explain. But it's only a matter of time before we fill in the gaps of human knowledge. I can't see where the concept of God adds anything to our understanding of the world, or how God would be relevant to my life."

Kimi had been listening politely to Tai. Now she spoke . . . her voice barely more than a whisper.

"Mr. Tai. I have seen God. And felt God. He is here with us now.

His existence is – what did the man say? – 'self-evident' to me."

"Could you point Him out to me, please?" Tai said sarcastically, and in my view, with unnecessary cruelty.

Kimi did not allow Tai's sarcasm to irritate her. They say that still waters run deep. Kimi was proving to be a pool of stillness. I felt a paternal fondness for the young woman.

In response to Tai's comment, Kimi raised her arms slowly at her sides.

"He is in the air that sustains us, without which we could not live."

She brought her hands close to her chest.

"He is in my heart and my mind. He guides my thoughts and my actions. He is in all living things. His breath moves the wind. His fire lights the sun. He moves the waters from the oceans to the sky and back again.

"He is in my brothers and sisters in this room."

She looked the scowling Tai directly in the eye.

"He is in your eyes also, Mr. Tai . . . though you have buried Him deeply – so deeply that you are blinded to His presence."

Tai reacted by turning away from the diminutive Kimi, his legs and arms crossed in Clete's direction. He looked at the ceiling and said to no one in particular, "This is voodoo bullshit!"

"I see what I see, Mr. Tai. I know what I know. I am sorry that this distresses you."

Kimi's voice remained soft and genuine.

Tai turned back toward Kimi, hostility in his eyes. I prepared to intervene if necessary.

"Listen, Pocahontas. God doesn't blow the wind. Changes in air pressure do. And the water returns to the clouds through a basic scientific process called e-vap-o-ra-tion."

His manner repulsed me.

"It rains when the humidity in the clouds becomes too great to retain all the water vapor in the air. Sorry little girl. There's no room for your God in the real world. His purpose died with your honored ancestors."

"All right now, Tai." It was Clete. "That'll be enough of that. If you're claimin' to be civilized, you're sure not actin' like it. Didn't your mama teach you any manners? Shame on you talkin' to a young lady that way. All she said was what she believes. And you get all defensive and mean.

"Shame on you! Shame!"

Way to go, Clete! I wouldn't have expected him to defend Kimi the way he did. Sometimes first impressions can be deceiving.

I needed to add my voice to support Kimi.

"Clete's right, Tai. You can't be attacking us for our beliefs. You can believe what you want . . . but keep your cool. Kimi was nothing but respectful to you. I think you owe her an apology so we can get back on track here."

"Damn straight!" Clete joined in.

Tai knew he had overreacted. You could see it in his face. But he was still angry, and now staring at the table top. Finally he mumbled, "Okay. I got a little hot. I'm sorry."

He took a deep breath and exhaled. Then he turned to Kimi.

"Miss, I am sorry for how I spoke to you. I was wrong. I will try to do better."

"Thank you, Mr. Tai," Kimi said.

Clete spoke again.

"Okay then. Let's get back to deliberatin'.

"Now I hear what your sayin', Tai, about science coverin' all the bases these days. Seems like if we can't explain some mystery right now, we'll be able to soon. So why do we need God? And I don't see him all around me like Miss Kimi does. But all that doesn't prove He ain't there.

"I got a feeling that before this trial is over, all our heads are gonna be spinnin'. So I plan to decide this trial the same way I've made every successful business decision in my life. If there's a way to guarantee a win, I'm gonna take it. Here's how I got it figured.

"If I vote for 'No God,' and it turns out there is a God after all, then God's probably gonna be pissed at me. I sure don't need that. On the other hand, if I vote that there *is* a God, and it turns out there isn't – no loss.

"So pretty much no matter what they say in that fancy theater room, I'm gonna vote 'Yes' for God.

"Makes sense, don't it?"

My turn to speak.

"Clete. I follow your logic. I'm just not sure we can all make this decision that easy. What if you vote for God, but God knows you're just hedging your bets, and that you really don't believe what your vote is saying? And He thinks you're trying to play Him? Where does that leave your approach?"

I didn't wait for Clete to respond.

"Don't get me wrong," I said to everyone. "I'm not saying Clete can't choose his own way to vote. That's up to him. But I've heard some very interesting arguments and evidence so far. And I'd like to know what you think about it. Can I bounce some questions off all of you?"

Clete and Tai nodded.

Kimi said, "Sure, Mr. William."

I viewed this trial as an intellectual exercise. I would approach it as I would have any client's legal problem.

"Help me think this one through. What if God is showing himself to us in the complexities of the human body, for instance? And because we think we pretty much understand the human body, we're overlooking the fact that it's pretty damn amazing.

"Even though we know a lot about humans, we can't make a person from scratch. Maybe we can clone one, or insert some sperm into an egg. But we can't start with algae and a chemistry set and make a person.

"Are we assuming too much because we believe we can understand everything? What if there are some things the human mind can never comprehend?"

Tai dove in.

"Okay. I'm going to try to stay calm. But here's what I would say to your question. Why do we *want* to make humans from algae? We can cover the whole human-making process with the tools we already have.

"We can do test tube fertilization and implant the fertilized egg to grow a baby that way. If we can't do so already, we'll soon be able to make endless duplicates of any human we choose through cloning. And we can grow spare body parts by giving genetic instructions to stem cells – of which there appear to be a very large supply now that fetal stem cells aren't the only ones we can use. And of course there's always good old-fashioned sexual reproduction.

"Who cares about making humans from algae or amoebas or whatever? We don't need God to make humans. Why do you care?"

"I can see," I said to Tai, "that you take a pragmatic approach to this issue. I'm trying to think beyond the practical for the moment.

"My real question is whether we are letting our own abilities and understanding blind us to what truly amazing things God may have done? I'm not saying God did anything at all at this point. I'm just asking us to examine our perspective.

"Kimi sees God in the wonder of His creation. Maybe we should consider whether we aren't blinding ourselves to that wonder . . . . Just throwing that out for discussion."

Tai: "You're not making any sense to me, man. I'm sorry. I just don't get at all where you're coming from."

Clete: "I kinda see what y'all are sayin', Bill. How our eyeballs let us see stuff. How our brain lets us think, and our heart lets us feel. It's all pretty deep stuff, ya know. I'm not saying you don't raise a good point. But settin' my vote aside for the minute, I'm not buyin' a God in all of it just yet."

Kimi: "Mr. William. You ask why I see God and some others do not. It is good to ask this question. I know God because I have always known Him. Perhaps my life experiences are different from others. I do not know these things. I am only saddened that I cannot share my sight with everyone."

Clete: "As long as we're talkin' philosophical, what about the stuff the second Witness said about God not bein' able to make a rock He couldn't move?"

Tai: "And how can there be free will if God knows our every decision before we make it? He mentioned that, too. Seems like the God he was talking about would be logically impossible."

Kimi: "I cannot answer for all of you. But for me, God, the Great Spirit, Wakan Tanka, is able to do all things. I believe He can make a rock He cannot move and be able to move it at the same time – though I cannot explain it."

Tai: "That's just stupid."

Clete and I gave Tai a stern look.

Tai: "Okay. I'm sorry for my choice of words. But it *cannot* be possible for an object to be immovable and a force to be irresistible at the same time. Something's gotta give."

Clete: "I have to go with Tai on this one. Makes no sense that we have free will if God already knows what we're gonna do. How could we change our minds if it's already written in God's book somewhere?"

"I know," I conceded. "Those logic arguments sound pretty strong to me, too. And I'm not sure I can connect with what the woman lawyer meant when she said, 'What if the sacred tools of logic and reason are too dull?' It's an analogy I find hard to accept."

"Aw, hell, Billy Boy! I get that one plenty. Here's another way to think about it.

"S'pose I got around 10,000 head of beef cattle grazing on 25,000 acres of range. How would you go about figurin' out *exactly* how many head I got at any given time?"

"I'm not sure I understand," I said. "I guess I'd count them."

"Damn straight! That'd be using math as your 'sacred tool.'

"Okay. So you head out in your chopper to count them cattle. You kinda lay out a grid of land and start countin' the number of cows in each square as you fly over. But as you're movin' back and forth across them 25,000 acres, summa the cattle you already counted move outta their boxes and into one you ain't counted yet – or visa versa. Sure as anything, you're gonna either count some twice or miss some.

"Am I right?"

"I suppose so."

"So even though your 'sacred tool' is custom made for countin', this job is just too big for math to work right. You need somethin' more.

"I think the lady lawyer is sayin' the same thing about logic and reason. Maybe all by themselves, they just ain't up to the job of figurin' out God. I don't know if I believe it. But I think that's what she was tryin' to say."

"Interesting thought, Clete. I'll give that idea some more consideration. Thanks."

"No problemo, Billy Boy."

Clete's analogy was better than I had expected from the rough-hewn south-talker. Even though everyone would agree that math is the right tool for counting, by itself it couldn't deal with all the practical challenges posed by the large cattle ranching business. You'd never know *exactly* how many cows you had at any given time by counting alone. Mathematics was 'too dull' an instrument to tackle this question.

For a time, we were all silent.

Discussions, and sometimes shouting matches, continued around us. I still could not decipher their words.

Then Kimi finally spoke – her words aimed at the table top.

"I am sad that the God of your thoughts is so small."

CHAPTER 10
THE THEOLOGIAN

When returning to the Courtroom, we followed the same inexplicable seating procedures as before. The lawyers stood at their tables and the Court Officer left to summon the Judge.

As we waited, I noticed that my sense of time and place were – I don't know the best way to say it – losing their footing? The repeating cycles of the Assembly Room, our walks to and from it, the Courtroom, the interplay of light and darkness, the sense of wandering through time with no clock, watch, or light of day to provide orientation. I wondered if this was how a person in a sensory deprivation chamber would feel – isolated from the normal sensory inputs. Floating in space and time.

"All rise.

"Hear ye! Hear ye! This Court is now in session. The Honorable Judge Jonathon Cole presiding."

The Judge resumed his position on the Bench as he had on the previous occasions.

JUDGE: "Please be seated.

"Counsel for the Repudiation of God will call his next Witness."

The Witness Stand appeared from the darkness. It was occupied by a heavyset Caucasian man, his brow perspiring noticeably. His name was indecipherable, but his credentials, once again, were top notch. His expertise was in theology – the study of God and religion.

COUNSEL FOR REPUDIATION: "You are presently employed as

a Professor of Theology at Southwest Baptist Bible College, is that correct?"

WITNESS: "Yes."

COUNSEL: "Could you please describe the life route that led you to your current occupation and beliefs about God?"

WITNESS: "Certainly. I am asked to recount the story often."

He settled himself in the Witness chair.

"I had what I would consider my first truly religious experience at age fourteen. I was confirmed as a member of an Evangelical Christian Church and accepted Jesus as my Lord and Savior.

"As a teen, and throughout my college years, I studied the Bible zealously. I sought to squeeze the true meaning from every word. I knew that the Bible held God's own voice, and I wanted to hear Him clearly.

"Upon graduation from college, I attended Harvard Theological Seminary where I earned both a Masters of Divinity and a PhD in Theology. It was during my studies at Harvard that my theological pursuits began to pull me away from the religion of my youth.

"At that time, I had set as a goal for myself to determine the definitive texts of all books of the Biblical New Testament. I wanted to confirm God's precise words to man.

"I learned to interpret and translate original Biblical materials written in Hebrew, Greek and Aramaic. As I delved into the ancient manuscripts, the huge number of discrepancies in their accounts astounded me. Nevertheless, I remained certain that there must be two or more scrolls from different sources that would coincide with one another to establish a definitive translation of *The* Bible.

"Consistent texts continued to elude me. The more I read, the more errors I found.

"I continued my research. But no matter how many scrolls I studied, I was not getting closer to a convergence upon a definitive Bible.

"Further research convinced me that many of the 'errors' I had identified in the texts were not mistakes at all. They were intentional alterations. Some changes had originated with church leaders at the time of transcription. Others were the work of scribes who sought to impart their own meanings to Biblical teachings. In each case of alteration, the perpetrator's motivation was to manipulate the message of the Bible for his own purposes.

"When I discovered this phenomenon of adulterated texts, I decided to catalogue the errors in the New Testament. Over the next several years, I sought out and read for myself many more original scrolls. Every single one contained altered material. No two were the same. I still could ascertain no definitive version of any scripture – none at all.

"If there was no way to discover the true text, the one version given by God's own inspiration, I had to conclude that the books of the New Testament were inherently defective, and could not be relied upon by modern Christians to accurately convey God's message to mankind.

"With this last conclusion came another disturbing revelation. If God could not, or would not, protect the integrity of the Holy Scriptures, He was a not a God in whom I could trust or believe.

"From that day forward, I have sought anew the truth of God's existence.

"I have yet to find it."

COUNSEL: "Are you alone in identifying these New Testament errors?"

WITNESS: "No. Many Biblical scholars corroborate my findings. Collectively, we have established the fact that, through the course of numerous translations and intentional alterations, a huge number of errors have infiltrated the original Biblical message – if there ever was one definitive message. The current New Testament definitively *does not* contain the text intended by its original authors."

COUNSEL: "Have you taken your findings to Christian scholars to hear their response to your concern about the Bible's accuracy?"

WITNESS: "Yes. Some have said the variations are mostly trivial. To which I respond that the infallible Word of God should not contain errors at all. And I further point out that the nontrivial errors are severely problematic.

"On one occasion, when I identified to him a particularly troubling discrepancy in the Book of Mark, a Theology Professor at a major University responded, and I quote, 'Maybe Mark just made a mistake.' That was not an answer I could accept.

"With contradiction compounding upon inaccuracy, and Christian scholars acknowledging the errors in the Bible, I could no longer call myself a Christian. The Bible is the Holy Book of the Christian Religion. It is the foundation for all Christian teachings. If it is riddled with errors, the Christian Religion is at best a collection of arbitrary assumptions, and at worst, entirely worthless babble.

"I could no longer have any part of it."

COUNSEL: "And since the time when you rejected Christianity, have you adopted any other version of a belief in God?"

WITNESS: "I have not. To my great disappointment, evidence supporting God's existence in the world seems to be sadly lacking. And indications of His absence are plentiful. Global terrorism is on the rise. Torture of untried enemy combatants and innocent civilian prisoners is increasing. Starvation and pandemics are the constant curse of the poor and downtrodden.

"It is difficult to see God in all this suffering."

COUNSEL: "You mention human suffering as evidence against the existence of God. My understanding is that the question of why God, if He is all-loving and all-powerful, allows so much pain and anguish in the world, is not a new subject. Both secular and theological scholars have debated this very issue for centuries. Am I correct?"

WITNESS: "You are correct."

COUNSEL: "What arguments do theologians make to explain this disturbing phenomenon?"

WITNESS: "Most commonly, the response to why God would allow so much suffering is that the pain is all part of God's greater plan. People need to have faith in that plan. Ultimately, the suffering will be shown to have been necessary, or at least beneficial, to achieving God's unfathomable goals. In short, we are asked to acknowledge that God's allowing of suffering makes no sense to humans. But we should have faith that suffering and pain, which appear hurtful and cruel to us, are parts of something good in God's eyes.

"That explanation is nonsense to me. You are what you do.

"If God allows all of us to suffer in varying degrees, and in diverse, and some might say perverse, ways, God is *not* loving. Period. I can have no faith in such a demonstrably unloving and uncaring God, and therefore, find it highly unlikely that God exists.

"Another fairly typical response to the preponderance of suffering in the world is to say that it is man's free will that causes the suffering – not God's desires. There are several critical errors in this line of thinking.

"First of all, if God is all-powerful, it does not matter the source of the suffering, He could alleviate the anguish if He so chose. What loving parent would not protect his or her child from any amount of suffering if it was within their ability to do so?

"But God does not abolish suffering. Therefore, He is as much to blame for it as any human free-will that may have contributed to the problem.

"Second, it is manifestly clear that not all suffering is of human origin. When earthquakes devastate the lives of thousands upon thousands of people . . . when hurricanes, tsunamis, tornadoes, wildfires, floods and other natural disasters wreak havoc in the lives of men, women and children alike . . . can man's free will be blamed for the suffering? Of course not.

"To my mind, the only reason that a loving God would not intervene to prevent the pain, devastation and anguish such natural disasters inflict on humankind is that He does not exist. Very few humans, if they were able to prevent it, would allow such damage and destruction in the lives of others. How could there be a God, whose love should be infinitely greater than the love of humans, who would allow this indiscriminate suffering to crush His children?

"If there is such a God, I do not want to know Him."

The attorney allowed a long pause for these last statements to rest heavily upon the Jurors. I knew this technique. It could be a very effective one, in the right circumstances.

COUNSEL: "Thank you, Professor." Then to the Judge, "I am finished examining this Witness."

The lawyer returned to his table and Counsel for Existence took her stance in the lit circle.

COUNSEL FOR EXISTENCE: "Good day, Professor."

WITNESS: "Hello."

COUNSEL: "Well. You have certainly given us much to think about."

WITNESS: "I can imagine."

He was starting to sound fairly impressed with himself.

COUNSEL: "Will you indulge a few questions into your background and life experiences, so the Jury may better assess the testimony you have just given?"

WITNESS: "Of course. I have nothing to hide. Ask your questions."

COUNSEL: "Thank you.

"Now Professor, you were raised in a Christian home. Correct?"

WITNESS: "Yes."

COUNSEL: "Both of your parents were faithful Christians and your family attended church on a regular basis?"

WITNESS: "Yes."

COUNSEL: "Is it fair to say that throughout your youth, and continuing into your college years, you considered yourself a Christian – a person who had faith in the Christian God?"

WITNESS: "The foolish faith of an immature youth, yes."

COUNSEL: "I understand that your family had some challenging times during your teenage years. Among other concerns, your mother was diagnosed with breast cancer when you were fifteen years old. Is that correct?"

WITNESS: "My mother had cancer. Yes."

He shifted awkwardly in his chair.

COUNSEL: "And her doctors treated the cancer aggressively. They removed both of her breasts in a radical double mastectomy. But the cancer had spread to her lymph nodes as well. So after the surgery, they gave her both radiation and chemotherapy in an attempt to eradicate the remaining cancer.

"This time of her illness must have been very difficult for your family."

WITNESS: "Yes."

COUNSEL: "Your mother was either in the hospital, at home in bed, or barely had the energy to function around your home, for a period of more than two years. She endured a good deal of pain, nausea and general suffering as a result of the cancer and the side effects of her treatment. True?"

WITNESS: "Of course. It was a tremendously painful and exhausting time for my mother."

Irritation had begun to seep into his voice.

COUNSEL: "And for your family as well."

WITNESS: "Yes."

COUNSEL: "Finally, more than two long years after the discovery of the cancer, the doctors declared it in remission. Essentially, she was cured. Even then it took many months for her to regain her strength. And there was no way you could really know the extent of her psychological anguish at the loss of her breasts.

"All true?"

WITNESS: "Her recovery was long and challenging, as I have already acknowledged. And no, I could not read her mind concerning the mastectomy."

COUNSEL: "And being a devout Christian family, all of you no doubt did a lot of praying during the time of your mother's illness, treatment and recuperation."

WITNESS: "We and numerous others. Many members of our congregation prayed for Mother's healing as well. But her recovery was the result of good medical care – not divine intercession."

COUNSEL: "Is that what you believed at the time?"

WITNESS: "I'm not sure . . . I believe so . . . yes."

COUNSEL: "So when your mother was cured and your family had survived this extreme trauma, was it at that time that you decided God was too cruel to be a loving God? Or did you come to that belief many years later?"

The Witness waited a moment before answering.

WITNESS: "I see what you are trying to imply here. You want me to say that I accepted my mother's suffering and yet retained my Christian faith.

"Well, I suppose that is true. But as I have already pointed out, my faith at the time was the product of an immature, preconditioned, teenage mind."

Counsel paused before continuing.

COUNSEL: "Actually, I was wondering whether you found your faith to be a comfort to you during this difficult time in your youth?"

The Witness tried again to find a comfortable sitting position.

WITNESS: "To be completely honest . . . and that is what I have been at all points during this testimony . . . I confess that I *did* find comfort in my illusion of faith. It was the sort of comfort that a young child receives from a baby blanket, or an infant derives from a pacifier. It was a false comfort based on a fallacious belief that God was holding our family in His hands and would see us through the turmoil of Mother's sickness."

COUNSEL: "But He *did* see you through that difficult time."

WITNESS: "No. Doctors, friends, family members . . . were with us. But we made it through all on our own."

COUNSEL: "I want to be clear about this. As I understand your testimony, you felt comfort from your faith while your mother was ill, but you now attribute that comfort to delusion – to false beliefs. Is that a correct restatement?"

WITNESS: "I thought at the time that I felt comfort in faith. But I was deluding myself. *That* would be a correct restatement."

He was now sounding patently hostile.

COUNSEL: "I apologize that my questions seem to be causing you some anxiety. But the Jury needs to understand you, your faith, the loss of your faith, and the underpinnings of your present self."

Her voice was calm, comforting, genuine.

COUNSEL: "I do need to ask just a few more questions about your family's religious beliefs – the beliefs that formed your 'immature faith,' as you have called it."

The Witness had managed to calm himself. He no doubt realized that his combative demeanor would not win converts to his cause.

WITNESS: "I understand. Go ahead."

COUNSEL: "Your family belonged to a church that most people would consider a 'Fundamentalist Church.' Is that accurate?"

WITNESS: "Yes. In fact, we took pride in being considered fundamentalists, because being devoted to Christian fundamentals means being focused on the most basic, universal and important tenets of the Christian Religion. Not deviating from God's true path.

"The more I think about it today, the more I am embarrassed by the foolishness of it all."

COUNSEL: "Is a literal interpretation of the Bible one of the 'important tenets' of fundamental Christian Religion that you just mentioned?"

WITNESS: "Yes."

COUNSEL: "So in your youth . . . during the immaturity of your intellectual development . . . if the words of the Bible said, for instance, that anyone who failed to accept Jesus Christ as his personal savior was going to hell, that was what you believed. Is that accurate?"

WITNESS: "That is correct. And your example is a fine one. It states precisely one of my former church's fundamental beliefs."

He was trying to regain points with the Jury by being more cooperative and complimentary to the lawyer.

COUNSEL: "So studying the literal meaning of the Bible was important to your faith at the time."

WITNESS: "Yes."

COUNSEL: "As you grew older, you carried your Biblical studies to the deepest and broadest extent possible. You learned the ancient languages in which scribes had recorded Biblical texts. You sought out and examined hundreds of such texts, searching for God's ultimate truth in the actual words He had inspired the Bible's first authors to write. You became such an expert in the area of Biblical history and translation, in fact, that very few humans on earth possessed your understanding of Biblical origins and transformations. All true?"

WITNESS: "There are certainly other Biblical scholars. But from an objective viewpoint, few have devoted as much scholarly time and intellectual effort to understanding the Bible as I have. I know that sounds a bit vain. But it is a fact."

COUNSEL: "So when, in the course of your extensive study and research of the Bible, you found that the literal words of the original scribes could not be ascertained with any degree of certainty, how did you feel? I mean, the Bible itself . . . one of the pillars of your religious faith . . . had been nullified, made useless by those who sloppily, or with misguided intent, inaccurately transcribed or improperly translated Biblical texts.

"That must have been a devastating experience."

WITNESS: "I don't know if devastating is the correct term. Surprising. Shocking. Disheartening. Those things, certainly."

COUNSEL: "And so, upon attaining the unavoidable truth that the Bible in its current incarnation does not contain the literal words of the original authors – words supposedly inspired by God, to be written and rewritten verbatim throughout time – you had no choice but to abandon your Christian faith and denounce the Bible."

WITNESS: "Yes. It would be ridiculous to base a faith in God upon a horribly flawed and damaged document, the true source of which could never be determined.

"Of course, I abandoned my faith."

Counsel turned toward the Jury.

COUNSEL: "Of course."

WITNESS: "That's what I said."

He was sounding argumentative again.

Counsel now returned her direct attention to the Witness.

COUNSEL: "At one time in your life, when you were a boy – and even when you were a young scholar well into his twenties – you believed that the Bible was the holy word of God, inspired by God Himself. Man's hand merely transcribed God's literal words – acted as his scrivener. To quote the King James Version of the Second Book of Peter: 'Holy men of God spake as they were moved by the Holy Ghost.'

"That was what you once believed. True?"

WITNESS: "Yes. And I will reiterate that I now consider such belief to have been foolhardy and ignorant."

COUNSEL: "So you have made eminently clear.

"Was the infallibility of scripture also your belief at the time you began searching for the 'authentic' Bible – the texts inscribed by the original authors of its books?"

WITNESS: "Yes, it was. Ironically enough, I was actually trying to ensure the Bible we were studying in the current century was historically correct. No one was more shocked than I was when I discovered the travesty of it all."

COUNSEL: "If I understand you correctly, at one time you had a faith that allowed you to believe that God could inspire prophets and scribes to write His exact words. Correct?"

WITNESS: "Yes."

COUNSEL: "And yet, at the same time, your faith would not allow for a God who could inspire the *readers* of the Bible to understand His teachings as set forth therein, regardless of human meddling in their translation.

"I find this puzzling.

"I mean, God must have known from the outset that the original scriptural texts would need to be translated into many languages. Since exact translation between different languages is not humanly possible, He must have anticipated the need for some modifications to His divine words. He certainly did not expect only those who could read Hebrew or Aramaic to have access to his 'Word' – a pillar of the Christian religion, as you have called it.

"Isn't it possible that God allowed, and possibly even guided, the multiple variations in the Biblical texts to meet the needs of its readers throughout history – so they could understand Him more clearly?"

WITNESS: "No. It is not possible. If He existed, God would not have allowed humans to meddle in His plans – not to deface an instrument as crucial to faith as the Bible."

COUNSEL: "You are not hearing me, Professor. What if the alterations to the Bible were actually made *by* God? By men acting with His divine inspiration? And not by meddlers as you suppose."

The Witness gave no response.

COUNSEL: "When you chose to leave the Christian Church, was your faith too small to allow God to act in this way? Or was it your God that was too small."

Kimi's words echoed in my head.

The Witness had worked himself into a lather.

WITNESS: "God's size is not at issue, Madam. It is his very existence I question. Reliable research brings that existence into serious doubt. I have simply accepted the facts as I found them."

COUNSEL: "I see.

"I apologize for the anxiety I have caused you, Professor. I honestly do. But it is said, you know, that the truth hurts. Perhaps it hurts most when it can do the most good. Personally, I believe that to be the case.

"I wish you nothing but the best in your struggles, and pray that one day you will return to the 'foolish' faith of your youth."

WITNESS: "Young woman, your twisting of my arguments will have no effect on the Jury's ability to find the truth in this matter. The facts will speak for themselves."

COUNSEL: "Which facts would those be, Professor? The facts

that prove you hold a rigid and narrow definition of God? Or the facts that prove God's ability to transcend human attempts to stuff Him into the box of their choosing?"

Again, the Witness gave no response.

COUNSEL: "No more questions for this Witness, Your Honor."

Counsel calmly took her seat.

The Judge turned to the male attorney whose light was now glowing at a medium intensity.

"Redirect, Counsel?"

COUNSEL FOR REPUDIATION: "Thank you, Your Honor."

The light circle increased to full brightness as the male attorney approached the Witness.

COUNSEL: "Professor. After that lengthy cross-examination, I need you to remind me about the substance of your original testimony. Was it something about the Bible and some errors?"

WITNESS: "Yes. All current translations of the Bible are riddled with errors. There are more so-called 'original texts' of each Book of the New Testament than there are words in the Books themselves. Any message contained in a modern-day Bible is purely a message from human to human. The Bible is worthless as a religious resource."

COUNSEL: "And since all of Christianity is based entirely on the Bible's teachings . . . ?"

WITNESS: "Christianity cannot be classified as a legitimate religion. Its God has been made up by men. Its holy book is the result an indecipherable hodgepodge of often-misguided, human-inspired, philosophies."

COUNSEL: "And regarding the subject of God and human suffering?"

WITNESS: "The extent, duration and severity of human anguish are totally inconsistent with the existence of any loving God – and particularly inconsistent with the God of Christianity."

COUNSEL: "Thank you, Professor."

The Witness was excused in the usual manner – by turning out the light on the Witness Stand.

CHAPTER 11
TESTIMONIALS AGAINST GOD

The Jurors now sat in nearly total darkness – the only lighting in the room being the ever-present glow of the Judge and his Bench.

"At this time," the Judge announced, as the light surrounding him increased in intensity, "we will hear testimonials from Witnesses who have experienced extreme suffering, and who believe because of this suffering, there can be no loving God. Counsel will not be asking questions of these Witnesses.

"Since this is a change in evidentiary format, I must ask that you give your full attention to the Witnesses as they speak. Do not expect further clarification from the attorneys."

The Judge turned in the direction of Counsel for the Repudiation of God, whose light now shone softly.

"Counsel. Please produce your Witnesses."

At once the Judge's light dimmed to its usual level, while Counsel for Repudiation remained bathed in shades of grey.

THE FIRST TESTIMONIAL

Without warning, in the midst of the dark space in the center of the Courtroom, where the lectern had previously stood, a woman appeared in a bright circle of light. Her skin was dark brown. Her attire included a head scarf to cover her hair, and an orangish-yellow linen wrap that, within its voluminous folds, enveloped her body all the way to her ankles. In one bony arm she cuddled a small, thin child. In the other she clutched a human skull.

"My name is Ambala. In my right arm I hold my youngest son, Abidemi. He is three years of age, but cannot walk for he is too weak."

Her speech was thickly accented with a native African dialect of some sort.

"In my left hand," she held out the skull, "I hold my husband, Gunju."

I could hear Jurors gasping in horror.

"Abidemi and I live, for now, in a refugee camp in the Province of Darfur in the Country of Sudan."

The woman took a moment to steady her voice.

"Gunju was murdered two years ago while defending our home and family from Janjaweed horsemen. As I and our five children hid in our home, the Janjaweed whipped Gunju with leather and stabbed him with sharp sticks until he could no longer stand and fight.

"Then the Janjaweed invaded our home and dragged my twelve-year-old son, Kamau, and his ten-year-old brother, Rutendo, outside. The demon horsemen took turns shoving the boys back and forth between them . . . striking my sons repeatedly. When the Janjaweed had finished their fun, they stood my two small boys, bruised and bloody, against the wall of our home.

"Then they shot my sons in the head."

Her voice caught as she spoke the final word. Tears began to well in her eyes. She stood that way for nearly a minute, obviously too distraught to continue.

At last, she spoke again, her tone, one of determination as she fought back the tears.

"My young daughters, Dayo and Eshe, the men bound to take with them as slaves, or worse. But they did not find Abidemi, for I had hidden him in a box behind our home."

The woman's face now bore the marks of defiance as she continued. Her voice increased in volume.

"Before the Janjaweed left, four of them stripped my clothes from me so I was naked. They beat and raped me in front of the others and before the eyes of my daughters. When they were through, they set our home to fire and rode away, dragging Gunju behind them, tied to one of their horses by a hemp noose about his neck."

She shook the skull at us.

"All the world has known of these horrors in Darfur for many years. Yet no one comes to save us from the Janjaweed. No one will stop these atrocities . . . or end this genocide."

She spoke with anger and frustration as the tears now flowed freely.

"We have prayed and begged and pleaded for salvation from our affliction. We are helpless to defend ourselves, our children. And no one will save us.

"Our food is very little. Our water makes us sick. Yet no help comes."

She paused again, searching our faces for . . . compassion? Or maybe salvation? Then she continued.

"If there is a God, He is the ally of the Janjaweed. This I know in my heart.

"Abidemi and I will live or die without a God to fight for us."

She paused.

"We have no other choice."

The bright circle around the woman disappeared in an instant, leaving only silence and blackness where she had stood.

I could hear the quiet sobbing of fellow Jurors and found myself on the edge of tears as well. Why anyone should have to endure the suffering Ambala had so vividly described was beyond my imagination. Could there be a loving God who would allow such undeserved anguish? My former ambiguity about God slipped toward anger and frustration.

Did my anger mean I did believe in God's existence, if only to cast blame upon him? I struggled with this conflict of emotion and intellect.

The silence and blackness from the front of the Courtroom

assaulted us for what seemed an eternity as we contemplated the tragedy we had just heard.

THE SECOND TESTIMONIAL

Just as suddenly as the first Witness had vanished, a second Witness now stood in her place. She was a blond teenage girl, though from her gaunt form, tired eyes and pasty makeup, she could have been much older. Her black micro-mini-skirt, cropped top and purple denim shrug jacket were the unmistakable attire of prostitution. She stood before us, swaying clumsily on four-inch heels.

When she first spoke, her voice was very small.

"My name is Jade. At least that's who I've become."

She took a deep breath and spoke more boldly.

"When I was born, Ma named me Jennifer. She thought it sounded fancy. I've got no damn idea why she thought my name should sound fancy. But there was a lot I never got about Ma."

"I never knew the sonofabitch who was my Pa. And Ma either wouldn't tell, or didn't know for sure."

The girl repositioned herself atop the high-heels, searching in vain for a comfortable position.

"Jennifer turned fourteen years old last week, though Jade is twenty. Jade has been walking these streets for a little more than nine months."

As she mentioned the streets, a night scene of dimly-lit, weathered brick apartment buildings and littered streets appeared around her. Cars cruised slowly behind Jade with music blasting and bass pounding in disproportionate intensity. A dog barked somewhere. The stench of longstanding decay filled the Courtroom.

These special effects were impressive. I searched anew for their source, without success. This street scene had to be a projection. But it appeared stunningly real.

"Do you wonder how Jennifer became Jade? Do you even care?"

"Most people don't. But I guess I'm supposed to tell ya anyway.

So here goes."

The street scene changed to the interior of a tiny, drab apartment with peeling paint and the pungent smell of body odor.

"Jennifer grew up in so many of these places they're all the same to her now," Jade said, waving her thumb over a shoulder at the apartment behind her. "And I guess Jennifer really didn't give a damn where Ma chose to live. Her life was a living hell wherever they went.

"Ma had lots of man friends – that's what she called them. Usually, they lived with us in whatever one-bedroom flat we were staying in at the time. Don't remember any of 'em ever having a job. We lived off Ma's welfare and whatever we could scrounge on the street.

"Anyway, Jennifer used to be a kinda cute kid. So she was probably seven or eight when Ma's man friends started diddling with her. I remember the first one of Ma's dirt-bag boyfriends who made Jennifer take off her clothes for him. Ma was gone somewhere while he ran his dirty hands over her body and she was forced to smell his foul odor.

"When Jennifer told Ma about it – after that first time – Ma slapped her in the face and told her not to bad-mouth her elders. After that, Jennifer knew to keep her mouth shut.

"For as long as I can remember, Ma's man friends used Jennifer as a play thing. Jennifer couldn't see that she had any choice. And I don't think she did. Ma wouldn't protect her. She had no place to go to live. Never saw no Social Services people 'round our place.

"So when Jennifer was thirteen, after a real bad beating from an asshole that told her to call him 'Daddy,' Jennifer left the flat and came to live here in the streets."

The night scene of slum life reappeared around the girl.

"After a few cold, hungry weeks of eating out of trash cans and sleeping under icy stoops, Jennifer met Linc. He took her under his wing . . . gave her a place to sleep . . . food to eat. And he never messed with her. Jennifer fell in love with Linc. She would do anything for him.

"But it turned out Linc wasn't interested in love. He used Jennifer to make money. He whored her out on the streets to anybody who'd pay fifty bucks.

"After only a week of walking the streets for Linc, Jennifer learned she had to watch out for herself. Turned out Linc wasn't no better than Ma's man friends.

"So Jennifer split. All the way 'cross town, to a neighborhood where Linc wouldn't find her. After running from Linc, that's when she changed her name to Jade."

'Jade' posed defiantly for the Jury.

"I'm a lot tougher than Jennifer ever was."

The transition back to Jade's persona was startling.

"Men don't use Jade. Jade knows what she wants . . . and how to get it. I can make two hundred a night easy. And I can pick and choose whose money I take. I got a regular supplier that gets me good deals on coke. Sometimes he'll even take a trade.

"I'm pretty set now.

"Got it made."

She choked on the last line. Tears began to streak her mascara. Her voice faltered.

"Jennifer's still kind of a mess, though. She wants Ma to love her. She wants God to take care of her and keep her safe and off the streets.

"She cuts our wrists and takes too much drugs for our own good. I tell her to cut out the shit. There ain't no God. And she ain't got no Ma.

"No way it can be no different. This is life. She's gotta stop screwing with us."

The girl had stopped crying and resumed her street-hardened stance.

"Jennifer can be a real pain in the ass."

The street scene vanished, and the circle of light went dark on Jade.

CHAPTER 12
THE THIRD DELIBERATION

After Jade's Testimonial, the Judge sent us back to the Assembly Room for 'reflection and deliberation.' At my table this time were Clete, Dariah and Ariel, the young woman I had met only briefly when the Judge had first laid our task before us.

At the time, Ariel had been upbeat, excited, ready for adventure. The girl who now sat at my table wore tear-stained cheeks and carried shoulders that sagged beneath an unseen burden.

This time around, the discussion at our table was devoid of commentary concerning the ridiculous nature of the proceedings, or the absurd task which we had been assigned. Everyone was taking his or her role seriously.

The Testimonials had been sobering. Only a cold-hearted narcissist could have listened to the stories we had just heard and not have been deeply moved with compassion for the speakers.

Ariel turned her desperate eyes toward me.

"How can God let those things happen? How could He?"

Ariel looked to me for an explanation. I had none to give. I slowly shook my head and showed her my palms. How could I even begin to answer?

When I offered no sign of providing relief, Ariel turned to Clete and Dariah.

"How?" she begged. "Please tell me how?"

There was a long silence in our group as Ariel kept searching our faces for an explanation, for some glimmer of comprehension she might lack. Atop the table, Clete placed a hand on Ariel's forearm. Then he spoke to her. Calmly. Reassuringly.

"There, there, little lady. Just take yourself a deep breath now. Let your thoughts settle a bit. You shoulda never had to see all that . . . not at your age. That wasn't right."

It wasn't right! Why in the hell was this kid on a jury anyhow? Let alone this one?

Ariel took Clete's advice and tried to breathe deeply – her first few attempts halted by intermittent sobbing. But eventually, the breathing helped and she was able to shake the panic from her face.

"Now jus' remember to keep on breathin', Missy. Whenever you feel your guts up in your throat, make yourself breathe. You'll be all right. You'll be jus' fine."

Clete gave Ariel's arm a light pat, then withdrew his hand.

"I think all of our emotions have been laid a bit bare by the scenes in there," I said. "Let's take whatever time we need to process our feelings before we, ah, deliberate. Okay?"

The others nodded agreement.

Dariah produced her prayer book and began reading and head-bobbing. Ariel crossed her bare arms on the wooden tabletop and rested her forehead on them. Her eyes seemed to be closed. Clete leaned back in his chair and breathed intentionally, in and out, in a slow rhythm. His eyes were closed, too.

All at once I became acutely aware that I was not dealing with my own emotional outrage. Instead, I was stuffing it down inside me while I tried to focus on the legal business at hand. Intellectually, I knew addressing emotions by burying them in this way could lead to long term psychological problems. I tried to focus on how I felt about the mother-and-son Darfur refugees and the sexually-abused teen prostitute.

It wasn't easy for me.

I felt sorry for their suffering, certainly. I wished I could make everything better – whatever that meant. In the end, I was most disturbed by my own inability to access more empathy for their situations, to feel more directly the pain of their plights, to turn to my religious upbringing for insight.

Was I less compassionate than my fellow Jurors? Was I self-absorbed? Had I suffered my own version of emotional damage and buried it in my psyche? I supposed I wasn't going to find the resolution to my own stunted emotions at this table today. So I mostly waited for the others to be ready to discuss.

After several minutes, first Clete, then Dariah ceased their contemplations. We all waited in silence until Ariel raised her face from the table, placing her hands in her lap.

"Were you all waiting for me?"

"No, Darlin'," Clete replied. "We were waitin' for all of us. And now it seems we're ready."

I thought I would try to make sure we started our conversation on solid footing.

"Since the last deliberation, we've heard the Bible expert tell us that all current translations of the Bible are fatally flawed . . . that no New Testament Book actually represents the true words of its original author. He concludes that Christianity as a religion, since it is fundamentally based on the Bible's New Testament, is really not a religion at all – more of a human-inspired philosophy.

"Then we heard the powerful Testimonials from which we have all been recovering, the point of which was that no almighty and loving God would allow His children to endure such suffering. The speakers had concluded that there is no God.

"Does anyone have anything to add to that summary?"

"I believe you have covered the essentials," Dariah said. "I have nothing to add."

Clete and Ariel also seemed satisfied.

"Shall we talk about the Biblical scholar first? Maybe let our emotions recover before we address the Testimonials?" I suggested.

"Good idea," said Clete. "Here's my two cents.

"I think that Bible Perfessor needs to get his head outta the books and texts and scrolls or whatever, and wake up and smell the coffee. Those books had to be translated into English for us to read 'em. No translation is ever gonna be perfecto.

"I agree with the lady lawyer. His definition of God is outta whack. He prob'ly started out in the right direction and just lost sight of where he was tryin' to get to in the first place. Now he's a little too fulla himself to change his stance.

"Now I'm not sayin' that just because this guy's a little off the beam, he still may not be right that there ain't no God. There's still a lotta thinkin' to do before I'm willing to answer that one. I just don't believe that because he reads Hebrew and God knows what else, that he's qualified to tell God – if there is a God – how to write His Holy Book."

"But if we can't believe that what the Bible says are God's words, then whose words are they?" Ariel asked. "And what *can* we believe?"

I decided to add my opinion.

"Ariel. I know having a highly-educated and well-respected biblical scholar tell you something can make it pretty easy to believe what he's saying. But if we do what the lawyers reminded us is our job – listen to evidence and make our own decisions . . . don't let the Witnesses make our decisions for us – then what does the Professor's testimony really boil down to?

"The evidence he presented is that the exact wording of ancient Bible texts has changed as it has been copied and translated. It's not the original words God told somebody to write down. The rest of his testimony is conclusions.

"'We can't have Christianity if the Biblical texts aren't exact' – a conclusion. 'We can't believe that *anything* in the Bible comes from God because the translation is not what the Professor considers to be precise' – another conclusion. 'Humans made up Christianity.' Those are all conclusions.

"That's not his job – to draw conclusions. That's our job.

"His only evidence is that the wording of the Bible has changed through various translations.

"I think it *had* to change.

"Look at it this way. If you and I were living less than even five hundred years ago, we'd be talking with a lot of 'thees' and 'thous' and 'hithertos" and 'begats.' Those words are hardly used at all today.

"And that's just a few examples of changes over the last few *hundred* years. The texts the Professor is talking about were written maybe fifteen hundred years or more ago. Imagine trying to understand how they were speaking. Heck, English wasn't even a language back then.

"So Ariel, I'm with Clete on this one. It just makes no difference to me if the words are exact. And I didn't hear that the meanings were all changed around or anything . . . just the words themselves. If there is a God, and He wants us to understand the Bible today – not a thousand years ago – the words *have* to change. Don't you think so?"

Ariel was doing her best to take in this line of argument. She still looked unsure of what we were saying.

"Ariel. What do I mean if I say, 'Katie bar the door?' Or how about 'Let's head down to egg harbor and trip the light fantastic." Do you have any clue what those phrases mean?"

She shook her head.

"Those terms were popular at various times during even the last *one hundred* years. Language changes all the time. I don't think we should get too hung up on different wording in the Bible that only makes it more understandable to us today."

"Okay," Ariel said finally, not sounding convinced. "But what about the parts that the Professor said were real changes in meaning? How can we know which those are? I have to be able to trust that the whole Bible is God's word, not just most of it. Don't I?"

"Why do you believe in your God, Ariel?"

It was Dariah. She spoke with quiet assurance.

"Because I have faith, I guess. I learned about him and . . . and I just . . . believe, because it feels right. God feels real to me. I know He hears my prayers."

"Do you trust God to be honest with you?"

"Of course. Why wouldn't I?"

"Then why would your God let the Bible mislead you? Either you believe or you do not believe. If you believe, then you know there are some things you cannot understand. And you know there are false prophets who will try to trick you and twist God's word.

"Do not let one man's words make your decision for you. Listen to everything. But believe what you know to be true, and discard that which you know to be false.

"Does this seem right to you, Ariel?"

Dariah had given this issue a lot of consideration. I thought that was interesting since she is Muslim and doesn't even follow the Bible's teachings. As far as her faith goes, she wouldn't care if the New Testament was a fiction novel.

But her observations transcended sectarian boundaries. And I could find no fault with her approach. Any belief in God was going to require a leap of faith at some point. I could already see this from the trial evidence I had heard so far. Much more, and certainly contradictory, evidence would be coming when Counsel for God's Existence presented her case.

"God does seem right. He *feels* right. Thank you, Dariah. You sure seem to know God. Thank you again."

Ariel's words were sincere, and her voice had attained a calmness and composure beyond anything she had thus far displayed.

To help Ariel understand, Dariah had abandoned logic in favor of faith. I knew it was a dangerous leap off the ledge of reason. But probably, it was a jump every Juror in the room would need to either make or decry before this trial was over.

"That's probably all the time we should take to discuss the Professor's testimony right now," I said, in an effort to keep things moving. I had no idea what time it was. But I didn't want this trial to drag on for days.

"What do we make of the Testimonials?"

Ariel was, again, the first to speak.

"It is so sad, what happened to those poor people. And no one should have to live the lives they have lived. But I was always told, 'God has a plan for everything.' I don't know what plan He has that those people needed to suffer. But I don't pretend to understand God. I see the pain – but I know it's got to be God's will."

Clete jumped in.

"I'm gonna have to disagree with you on that one young lady. There's no reason I can even imagine that justifies putting them folks through those . . . travails. If God can stop it, He should. To me the fact that He doesn't stop it is a darn poor reflection on any God that might exist. Darn poor reflection!"

Clete sat back in the wooden chair, arms across his chest. *'Nuf said!* As far as Clete was concerned, the discussion was over.

Dariah took up the exchange. Her tone was not disrespectful – but her voice was firm.

"Who are we to judge the ways of Allah? From dust we were made and to dust we will return. So it is written. All we have is from Allah. Shall we complain when He requires something from us in return?

"Please understand that I do not belittle the suffering of those people. Nor do I wish it upon anyone. But if such suffering occurs, there must be a reason – a divine reason humans cannot understand.

"This my faith tells me."

Well. I had heard two votes for "God must have a reason," and one vote for "There's no way God should let people suffer like that, if there is a God." I had given considerable thought to this 'suffering problem' for many years. This is what I had come up with.

"I see it this way . . . for what it's worth. If you believe God created humans with free will, then you can't blame Him when the humans start torturing each other. Could He stop it? Sure. But then free will goes out the window and God has an earthful of puppets, not people. Not created in his own image. Not possessing, and choosing to act upon, 'the knowledge of good and evil.'

"All of the suffering we heard described in the Courtroom – the horrible, sad, wretched, disgusting acts we heard recounted – all of them were directly caused by people . . . people exercising their God-given free will. God may have been able to stop the atrocities. But I will not lay the blame for them at His feet."

Clete was back on the edge of his chair, hands flat on the table. His mouth was open almost before mine had closed.

"That's the biggest bunch of B.S. I've heard in a long time. God coulda stopped the sufferin' and He didn't. What's His excuse? Was He 'just followin' orders'?

"Hell no! If He exists, God's as guilty as a soldier who stands by while women and children are murdered and does nothin', even though his rifle is at the ready. And He's as guilty as that young girl's mother who knows her boyfriends are screwin' her daughter, but doesn't throw 'em out and call the police.

"That's clear to me as the nose on your face. You can call him a co-conspirator, an accessory after the fact . . . hell, I don't care. He's complicit. His hands are dirty. That ain't no way for no God to act!

"Now I know this trial ain't over yet . . . but I'm rethinkin' my plan to vote for a God that has any part in the kind of sufferin' we heard about today."

Clete resumed his folded arms 'finality pose.'

Clete's tone had been pretty combative. And it didn't look like Dariah or Ariel was about to say anything to get him riled up. But I thought I'd try for a summation anyway.

"Well, Clete. I can certainly see where you're coming from. And you are absolutely entitled to express your opinion. In fact, maybe we should be indicting our own asses for failing to do anything to help those unfortunate souls in Darfur. But I'm still going to have to respectfully disagree that the existence of suffering in the world is reason enough to deny God's existence."

Clete began to lean forward.

"It's definitely a factor to be considered," I continued.

Clete leaned back again.

"But I'm still keeping an open mind until all the evidence is in. I've seen plenty of trials where, at the close of the prosecution's case, you'd swear the defendant was guilty. Then when the defense was done presenting its evidence, you had good reason to think otherwise.

"All I'm saying is – try not to make your mind up just yet. Let's wait 'til we hear everything – then decide."

"I s'pose you make some sense," Clete allowed. "But it's gonna take somethin' darn persuasive to make me change my mind."

I wondered what had become of Clete's 'guaranteed win' scenario, and whether it would re-emerge when he settled down.

I'm not sure if Dariah or Ariel had more to say, because just then, the Court Officer called us back to the trial.

CHAPTER 13
THE METAL WORKER

After we had assumed our new seats, following the usual, and indecipherable, seating prearrangement routine, the Judge re-entered the Courtroom, and Counsel for Repudiation called his next Witness.

From the initial questions, I gathered that this guy was supposed to be 'Mr. Regular Joe Atheist.' He was thirtyish. A sheet-metal worker with a high school diploma and some welding expertise – not at all the same sort of background possessed by previous experts.

I wondered what he would have to say.

COUNSEL FOR THE REPUDIATION: "Would you tell us please about your childhood experiences with religion, if any?"

WITNESS: "Yeah. No problem.

"I remember pretty well my parents draggin' me to church every Sunday morning. When I was really little . . . maybe five or something . . . they made me go to Sunday School first, and then sit through church afterward.

"That lasted 'til I got to be fourteen. Then I got confirmed. After that I just had to go to church. But it was every Sunday. And they dragged me outta bed whether I was tired, sick, or whatever.

"I'm pretty sure they thought they were doin' the right thing makin' me go to church like that. But usually, it was all I could do to stay awake between songs. When I was like a baby or something, they gave me Cheerios and coloring books to keep me busy so I wasn't too big a pain in the ass.

"Oops! Can I say that?"

COUNSEL: "As long as it's the truth."

WITNESS: "Yeah. I'm sure I was a pain in the ass, because I was bored as hell.

"Anyway, after I got past the Cheerios stage I had to just shut up and sit still or Mom would give me a whuppin' when we got home.

"I remember once we were sittin' in the balcony at church and I was leaning over the railing, pickin' my nose, and I flicked a booger off my finger. Mom jerked me back hard and told me the booger had landed on some guy's suit down below us. She said she hoped he wouldn't find out where it came from and I was gonna catch hell when we got home. Which I did."

He paused in his recitation.

COUNSEL: "Anything else you remember about church from your youth?"

WITNESS: "Well . . . there were lots of chants and stuff. After a while everybody would learn 'em so you could say 'em all together. And the organ music was really loud. And the Reverend used to stand up in the pulpit and tell us all how we were gonna go to hell if we didn't shape up and quit sinning so much. And by the way, we should make sure to be 'generous' when they passed the plate after the sermon."

COUNSEL: "Do you still attend church?"

WITNESS: "Hell, no."

COUNSEL: "When and why did you stop?"

WITNESS: "As soon as I graduated from high school I got a job and moved into a house with some other guys. Then Mom couldn't make me go to church anymore. So I quit goin'."

COUNSEL: "Have you had experiences with religion since you stopped going to church?"

WITNESS: "Whatta ya mean?"

COUNSEL: "For instance, have you had encounters or relationships with people who are religious or go to church?"

WITNESS: "Yeah. Sure. Almost everybody I work with at the shop claims to be Christian. A bunch of 'em go to church. Some all the time. And some just on holidays like Christmas and Easter.

"Oh yeah. Hey, I think this is kinda funny. My folks quit goin' to church now, too . . . 'cept for holidays and funerals. Guess they thought I needed religion more than they do."

COUNSEL: "And your contacts with co-workers haven't inspired you to return to church? Get back to your religious roots?"

WITNESS: "Ha! That's a hoot!"

COUNSEL: "Why do you say that?"

WITNESS: "Lotsa reasons."

COUNSEL: "For instance?"

WITNESS: "Well . . . for one thing, some of the guys that go to church real regular are the biggest damn jerks in the whole shop. One guy goes out drinking every day after work and tries to pick up whatever slut he can find at the bar. And he's married with two kids! But he puts his suit and tie on for church every Sunday. Guess the congregation thinks he's a pretty good guy 'cause they voted him to be on the church council. He reminds us that he's a church big-shot all the time at the shop.

"And one other guy who was always at my church when I was growing' up . . . he doesn't go so often anymore . . . anyway, he's the biggest liar and cheat I know. He talks behind everybody's back at work and gets everybody pissed at everybody else.

"Another guy keeps preachin' to me about how I should get to church and find Jesus, and how I'm for sure gonna burn in hell if I don't. He quotes Bible stuff at me and tries to make me feel like shit because I'm not takin' communion, or because I like to dance or play cards. Really weird stuff.

"Who ever heard of a religion that says you can't play cards? In my town there's a whole church chocked fulla people who claim that's what God says. And they're pissed at you if you disagree with 'em and like to deal a hand or two once in a while.

"And get this . . . their own goddamn Pastor, a married guy, got caught screwin' one of the parishioners. For Christ's sake! Their damn Pastor is one of the biggest sinners in the place. Ha!"

COUNSEL: "It sounds like you've met some Christians you're not too impressed with."

The Witness interrupted Counsel.

WITNESS: "Yeah. And for that matter, I ain't too impressed with Muslims tryin' to blow up planes, or Iranians wantin' to wipe out Israel. You see that stuff on the news all the time."

COUNSEL: "I understand that you now consider yourself an atheist. Is that correct?"

WITNESS: "If it means that I don't believe in God, yeah, that's right."

COUNSEL: "How did you come to the conclusion that there is no God?"

WITNESS: "Jesus! Haven't you been listening?

"Every so-called Christian I know is a goddamn hypocrite, pretending to be all pious and proper for an hour on Sunday morning, and then being a crook, or cheat, or something worse, all the rest of the time.

"Now I gotta admit that the only religious folks we got in my town claim to be Christian. So I don't have close-up experience with other religions. But it don't seem to me that the Palestinians, or the Iraqis, or the Jews, or the Pakistanis have got anything good goin' on neither. All they can think of is killin' each other. And mainly, it seems to me, they're killin' and hatin' each other because they have different religions. We get rid of religion altogether, seems like the world would be a whole lot more peaceful.

"The religion I've seen ain't for me. No thanks."

COUNSEL: "I have no further questions for this Witness, Your Honor."

As the lights dimmed on the male attorney and appeared on the female, in what I had come to consider a trivial and somewhat distracting ritual, I considered what the metal worker had to say.

His was not a 'thinkers' argument. More of a gut reaction. But I don't discount his testimony because of that. Gut reactions are often more reliable than over-thought conclusions. And his gut had been darn consistent throughout his testimony.

The female attorney was ready to begin her cross examination.

COUNSEL FOR EXISTENCE: "Please correct me if I'm wrong, but I'm hearing that you have two big complaints with religion.

"First of all, the people you know who claim to be religious are poor role models for human behavior. And second, you see religious institutions, organizations and governments around the world killing, threatening and warring over what they claim are religious convictions.

"Am I on track with those assumptions?"

WITNESS: "I'm not sure I follow you all the way. Let me take my own shot at summin' it up. Here's what I think. Religious people are hypocrites. Religious groups are killin' people right and left, and it seems their gripe is over religion."

COUNSEL: "Excellent summary. Thank you.

"Now, during the time you were living at home and brought up in a Christian church, do you remember learning anything about the teachings of Christianity – the teachings of the Bible?"

He ticked some points off on his fingers as he spoke.

WITNESS: "Don't kill. Don't lie. Don't steal. Don't commit adultery. Don't covet a bunch of stuff that ain't yours . . . whatever that means."

A few Jurors chuckled.

COUNSEL: "Those are some things the church taught you *not* to do. Do you remember anything that the church taught you that you *should* do?"

The Witness considered for a moment.

WITNESS: "Go to church on Sunday. Love people, even if they're mean to you. Do unto others as you want them to do unto you.

"I guess that's about all I remember."

COUNSEL: "It seems to me that you remember a lot of important things. Do you try to live your life according to those rules, or beliefs, you've just listed?"

WITNESS: "Mosta the time. Yeah. Sometimes it's hard for me to not get pissed at somebody who screws me over though. And I don't really believe in goin' to church on Sunday. That deal is just sort of a fund-raiser for the church."

COUNSEL: "I see. Let me ask you. Do you ever steal?"

WITNESS: "No."

COUNSEL: "Not even if it's maybe leaving some cash income off your tax returns?"

The Witness blushed.

WITNESS: "I guess I've maybe done that once or twice."

COUNSEL: "Or how about when the store clerk gives you too much change back from your purchase . . . do you keep that extra change?"

WITNESS: "I guess so. It's their fault for givin' it to me."

COUNSEL: "But is that how you would want to be treated if you were the store clerk, and the extra change was coming out of *your* paycheck?"

The Witness hung his head.

WITNESS: "I s'pose not."

COUNSEL: "How about lying? Do you ever do that?"

WITNESS: "Everybody lies. I guess I do . . . when I need to."

COUNSEL: "And how are you doing at loving the people who treat you badly?"

The Witness smiled.

WITNESS: "I suck at that one. But I don't sleep with other peoples' wives and I don't kill nobody."

COUNSEL: "So you admit that you believe it's wrong to steal and cheat, yet you cheat on your taxes and steal from store clerks. And you know you shouldn't lie, but you do so whenever it seems appropriate. And you believe you should love your fellow man, but you find it nearly impossible to do that when your fellow man treats you badly.

"It sounds to me like you buy into a lot of the beliefs of the

Christian church. And the values you have mentioned are, by and large, very similar to the beliefs of nearly every other religion as well.

"Nevertheless, you sometimes fail to act in a manner consistent with your beliefs.

"Can you explain why that is?"

The Witness squirmed in his chair. He was clearly unsure how to answer this question.

WITNESS: "No. I guess I can't. It just seems like sometimes . . . I just can't."

COUNSEL: "So do your failures to always comply with your beliefs make you a hypocrite, or a bad person?"

WITNESS: "Hell no! I do lots of good stuff, too. I'm a big brother for an orphan kid. And I coach a boys' basketball team. I do lots of stuff to help other people. Sure, I make some mistakes. But I'm not a bad person for it."

COUNSEL: "Please put yourself in my shoes for a moment. Let's say that I see you cheating on your taxes, and stealing from the clerk, and being mean, or at least less than loving, to your co-workers, should I conclude that, because you claim to be an atheist, atheism is a bad thing? Or that you are a hypocrite?"

WITNESS: "Neither one. I make mistakes. But I don't shove my beliefs down anybody else's throats. And I don't kill people because I'm an atheist."

COUNSEL: "I'm glad you mentioned that. Did you know that Adolph Hitler was an atheist? And Joseph Stalin?"

WITNESS: "No. I didn't."

COUNSEL: "Seems that both of them did a fair amount of shoving atheism down the throats of the Jews. The Holocaust and all. Don't you agree?"

WITNESS: "Yeah. I guess."

COUNSEL: "Would it surprise you to find out that, according to *The Encyclopedia of Wars*, less than 7 percent of all wars since the beginning of recorded history had any religious component whatsoever?

"And the United States, widely considered to be one of the more religious countries in the world, has been involved in a total of seventeen wars, only one of which – the War on Terror – had any religious connection at all?

"Should I conclude that atheism is the cause of most wars and therefore denounce atheism as a violent, war-mongering belief?"

I could tell the Witness was not used to being confronted with facts and figures. He was out of his element in this cross-examination. He squirmed and fidgeted and looked in the direction of the blackness of the Counsel Table to his left for help.

WITNESS: "No. If the people who started those wars were atheists, it wasn't their atheism that caused it."

COUNSEL: "Why? How can you say that?"

WITNESS: "Because atheists believe in peace and not in killing."

COUNSEL: "Just like Christians and Muslims and Jews and Hindi and Buddhists. All these religions believe in peace and forbid killing."

WITNESS: "Then the atheists who started the wars weren't actin' like the atheists I believe in."

COUNSEL: "It is interesting that you should say this. The same claim has been made for nearly every religious conflict in recorded history – including the War on Terror. The mainstream believers denounce the violence. But the extremists hijack religion and use it as their justification.

"It has long been said that every tyrant will find a pretext for his tyranny. Would you allow that maybe at least *some* of the 'religious wars' of which you have heard are, in fact, acts of tyrants using religion as their battle cry, and that the religions or religious institutions themselves are not really to blame?"

WITNESS: "I s'pose sometimes that might be true."

COUNSEL: "I have no further questions for this Witness."

She returned to the blackness awaiting at her Counsel Table.

The Judge spoke to Counsel for the Repudiation.

JUDGE: "Any redirect Counsel?"

A yellow light glowed at the Counsel Table where the male attorney sat. He stood to address the Judge.

COUNSEL: "No questions at this time, Your Honor."

JUDGE: "Then the Witness is excused."

The light went out on the atheist metal worker.

CHAPTER 14
THE FIRST COSMOLOGIST

JUDGE: "Please call your next Witness, Counsel."

The light brightened on the male lawyer as he stepped from behind his Counsel Table. A new Witness appeared in the now well-lit Witness Stand. He was an oriental man, perhaps forty-five years old, wearing a white cotton dress shirt with black shoes, socks and slacks.

COUNSEL FOR REPUDIATION: "Please state your name for the Court."

WITNESS: [Indistinguishable.]

Our inability to hear the Witnesses' names was beginning to irritate me. Why could we hear every other word with distinct clarity, but not the names? Not that a name should matter. Still . . . it bothered me.

COUNSEL: "Professor, what is your education and professional background?"

WITNESS: "I hold a PhD in mathematics from Duke University, a Master's Degree in Philosophy, also from Duke, and a PhD in Physics from Notre Dame. I am presently the Department Chair of the Physics Department at the University of Minnesota. I teach classes in particle physics and astronomy. My research interests lie in the area of cosmology."

COUNSEL: "And what is cosmology?"

WITNESS: "Cosmology is the study of the universe – its origin, structure, characteristics and development. One should be careful not to confuse cosmology with cosmetology, which has to do with hair, makeup and beauty treatments. Not at all the same thing."

There were a number of quiet laughs from the Jurors.

COUNSEL: "We'll be sure to keep that distinction in mind.

"So cosmology is the study of the Universe . . . pretty large topic, wouldn't you say?"

WITNESS: "About as big as they get."

COUNSEL: "I noticed you did not list any degrees in cosmology. Is there a reason for that?"

WITNESS: "To my knowledge, there are no accredited educational institutions offering degree programs in cosmology. Generally, cosmologists have educational backgrounds similar to mine – mathematics, physics, astronomy, philosophy and sometimes theology.

"You could say that cosmology is a cross-disciplinary pursuit. In some areas, knowledge of straightforward physics is applicable. But at the edges of cosmology lie issues of philosophy, theoretical mathematics and even theology – the origin of the universe being one example."

COUNSEL: " I realize this may be asking a lot considering the expansiveness of the subject matter, but do you think you could give us a brief history of the universe? To help focus your statement, I'd appreciate it if you could emphasize aspects of the universe that might speak to the existence or nonexistence of a God."

WITNESS: "Actually, the question of God comes up often in cosmology. So I believe I can accommodate your request.

"Let's start at the beginning. That's always a hot-button venue in religious discussions.

"For the past several decades there have been two predominating theories regarding the origin of the universe. The Solid State Theory and the Big Bang Theory.

"The Solid State Theory has been around for hundreds of years and maintains that the universe had no beginning and will have no end. It always was and always will be.

"The Big Bang Theory, in contrast, contends that the universe had an actual beginning approximately 13.7 billion years ago, and has been expanding ever since. Each of these theories has theological and philosophical implications. I will address the two theories separately if I may."

COUNSEL: "Please proceed."

WITNESS: "The Solid State Theory fits very well with Buddhism and other religions that maintain that we live our lives and are continually reborn, or reincarnated, over and over again, *ad infinitum*. And it fits well with the Theory of Evolution because it allows an infinite amount of time for complex organisms to mature from simple atoms and molecules.

"Many Christians, Jews and Muslims take exception to the idea that there was no beginning to the universe. Their Holy Books each contain a creation story where God forms everything out of nothing – interpreted as the creation of the universe.

"The Big Bang Theory, on the other hand, is a disappointment to Buddhists, and provides the other religions with at least an argument that, if there was a beginning to our universe, something must have existed before that beginning in order to cause the universe to come into existence. The predictable postulate from theologians is that God was the force that caused the universe to come into being.

"Scientific evidence in the form of deep space measurements of cosmic radiation, gravity patterns, interactions of celestial bodies, and other objective criteria seems to be mounting against the Steady State Theory, and in favor of the Big Bang. In fact, I feel quite comfortable saying that the Big Bang Theory is far and away the most widely supported view concerning the origin of the universe among scientists today.

"So now that we have settled on a theory to discuss, I will try to outline the basics of the Big Bang.

"According to this theory, everything we can see, feel, or detect by any means arose very suddenly out of a tiny, tiny speck composed of matter and energy. Some cosmologists refer to the point of origin as a 'singularity,' because we aren't sure how else to describe it.

"The singularity was a minuscule dot of infinitely small size and nearly infinite mass and energy. Its 'weight' was at least equal to all the mass in the universe. It also contained all energy in the universe.

"To ask where it was located is a silly question, because there was no universe in which to place it. It was, as far as we can tell, surrounded by nothingness. During the 'Big Bang' this singularity exploded in an unimaginably rapid expansion of space and time about 13.7 billion years ago.

"Incredible advances in astronomy over the past decades, like the Hubble Space Telescope and the COBE deep space radiation satellite, have provided concrete evidence of what the universe actually looked like about 12 billion years ago. The distances across space are so great that the light and cosmic radiation resulting from those ancient cosmological goings-on is just now reaching us. So we have a sort of time capsule for significant parts of the cosmos that has contributed greatly to our understanding.

"But no matter the sophistication of the technology, or the ingenuity of the scientists, we will never be able to go back in time to view the Big Bang occurring. We would have to be watching the creation event from a vantage point outside of our universe in order to observe its birth – an obvious impossibility.

"But we *are* able to observe galaxies, and even individual stars, as the universe grows. From those observations, we now know that the rate of expansion of the universe is increasing rather than decreasing, as scientists had previously believed. So it appears that the universe will continue to expand forever – until all the stars are so far apart that the night sky appears totally black to the observer.

"Of course, we will all be long dead by the time this occurs billions, or trillions, of years in the future. So let's not dwell on the end. Let's get back to the formation of the stars and planets.

"Near the beginning of the universe, the only matter existing was in the form of hydrogen atoms – atoms possessing only a single proton at their nucleus. As the hydrogen was burned in the solar furnaces of stars, including stars like our own sun, the intense heat fused the hydrogen into helium atoms – each possessing two protons – and released even more intense heat in this atom-combining process called 'nuclear fusion.'

"Some very large stars eventually became hot enough to fuse multiple protons together into larger atoms. Oxygen, nitrogen, carbon and silica, among others, are formed in this way. When these large stars self-destructed in tremendous nuclear explosions called supernovas, the larger atoms were launched across the galaxies and throughout space. Without stars becoming supernovas, the universe would never have been able to distribute these larger molecules which are critical to life.

"As the universe continued to expand, new stars formed from the cosmic debris of earlier supernovas, which combined with other stellar gases and repeated the process. Future supernova eruptions yielded even heavier atoms like iron, lead, uranium and many others.

"Ultimately, all complex atoms existing today on our planet, including those that form our bodies, were created in this way – assembled from the original basic building blocks of hydrogen atoms, and cycled through solar furnaces until they reached their present forms.

"Gravity was the force responsible for organizing the universe. It pulled the matter scattered through space by the Big Bang together into stars, planets, even galaxies. Eventually, gravity collected our own sun and planets together from remnants of what popular astronomer Carl Sagan liked to call 'star stuff.' Gravity continues to affect – to a large extent, control – the workings of the universe today.

"Moving from the cosmic perspective to a view a little closer to home, the Earth formed from rock fragments that were floating through space approximately 4.6 billion years ago.

"In its early years, the earth's surface was molten rock, probably fueled by the heat generated when smaller space rocks collided and fused together to form our planet. As each new rock melded into the molten earth, it added its own nuclear baggage of star-baked elements to our planetary storehouse.

"After a few million years, the earth's surface cooled and solid rocks began to form on the colder outer crust. Geologists have identified specific rocks dating back as far as 3.9 billion years. So we have strong evidence that the earth was at least partly solid by that time.

"Skipping forward nearly a billion years, life, in the form of single-celled organisms, first appeared in fossil records about 3 billion years ago. Microscopic life forms such as protozoa, fungi and bacteria apparently ruled the earth for the next billion years. There is no fossil evidence of more advanced life until about 1.9 billion years ago, when the single-celled creatures began evolving into more and more complex organisms.

"Eventually, through the evolutionary process, primitive humans arrived on the scene less than three million years ago – a mere blink of an eye in cosmological time. With the arrival of humans, another theological issue presented itself. If our human ancestors walked the earth millions of years ago, this fact contradicts the notion that the human time line began only several thousands of years ago, as interpreted from most Holy Books. For this reason, Darwin and his Theory of Evolution have been thorns in the side of religion ever since he introduced his theory in the late 1800s.

"The other religious concern is that Evolutionary Theory states that man had a string of living parents all the way back to the single cell organisms. This version of earth's history conflicts with the notion that God created man separately, and in his own image, as many religions profess."

The Witness, who thus far had been speaking mostly to the Jury, now turned to Counsel.

WITNESS: "Sorry. That got a little long after all, didn't it?"

COUNSEL: "That's okay. I prefer thoroughness over brevity.

"So let's go back to the first theological conundrum postulated by the Big Bang Theory. What about the argument that something had to cause the Big Bang, and that that something just might be God?"

WITNESS: "Can you see how we have made a segue from observational science – that is, provable scientific observation – into theory?

"I have already stated that scientists will never see the Big Bang happen. So all we have is theory to work with. Nevertheless, there are several theories that purport to address the issue of what happened at the very beginning of the Big Bang.

"One such theory I have already mentioned. Perhaps God, or a Godlike Being, set the universe in motion out of nothingness. That is precisely what several scriptural writings contend. It is certainly the position of the Judeo-Christian hierarchy . . . though they remain unhappy about the 13.7 billion year timetable.

"Theoretical mathematicians have come up with formulae that postulate some interesting alternative possibilities. According to mathematical models established by renowned physicists and mathematicians, all the laws of physics can be explained by something called 'String Theory.' You need a little history to see why 'String Theory' is needed.

"When Albert Einstein conjured up his Theory of Relativity – an equation many recognize as $E=mc^2$ – in 1905, it profoundly affected all aspects of physics. This mathematical equation has proven to be a very reliable predictor of physical interactions in the universe, and was considered the final word on the subject of the relationship between mass and energy until . . . subatomic physics came along.

"Some of the nuclear particles – the parts that make up atoms – that the physicists were finding wouldn't play along with results anticipated using Einstein's equation. So new theories needed to be developed to explain physical interactions on the subatomic level.

"Most of these theories are so complex as to defy simple explanation. Many involve more than three spacial dimensions . . . which makes them a non-starter from a common sense viewpoint. Who can visualize a dimension other than up, down or sideways? Our brains can't picture such a thing. Nevertheless, these multidimensional theories are mathematically viable, since mathematics is not constrained to three spacial dimensions. And each theory does successfully explain some of the observations scientists are making at the subatomic level.

"String Theory proposes an explanation that allows subatomic physics and Einstein's Theory of Relativity to connect, and to predict consistent results as one moves from the macrocosmic to the subatomic realm. String Theory postulates that there are up to ten spacial dimensions in existence, along with the single time dimension. But for some reason, seven of the spacial dimensions ceased their expansion a tiny fraction of a second after the Big Bang, while the other four dimensions – length, width, height, and time – have continued expanding.

"As I have already mentioned, quantum physics theories can make most people's heads spin. But I assure you that String Theory is a reasonable and scientifically testable model. It just requires highly sophisticated equipment and methods to test it. Such experimentation and testing is still a work in progress.

"According to String Theory, at the origin of the universe, time starts at zero, as do the other ten dimensions. When the Big Bang goes off, the clock starts running and all spacial dimensions expand – but only for the briefest of moments. After that very short time – the tiniest fraction of a second – only the four dimensions we humans can perceive continue expanding. The rest remain so closely bound in or around atomic nuclei that we cannot observe them.

"The possible existence of spacial dimensions we cannot explore has given rise to further discussions of God. Maybe He lives in one or more of those dimensions? Of course, if God lives in some dimension we cannot detect, we can't hope to find evidence of His existence. So this postulation may pose more questions than answers.

"There is also a newer theory – referred to as 'M Theory' – that purports to establish a sort of bubbling collection of expanding and contracting universes. It has some interesting aspects, but as yet, is not generally accepted as established science."

COUNSEL: "It is truly amazing to me, Professor, that you are able to comprehend the subject matter of which you have just so eloquently spoken. Given your deep understanding of the beginnings of the universe, what is your professional opinion about how the universe began?

"Was it 'caused'? And if so, by what?"

WITNESS: "At present, I have no professional opinion about causation for the beginning of the universe. Causation implies that one thing follows from another *in time*. Since there was no time at all at the birth of the universe, I'm not sure Newton's Second Law – that for every effect there is a cause – would even apply. I just don't have enough information.

"However, if I were to speculate about whether an almighty God created humans and made a nice cozy nest for them here on earth, I'd have to say that I'm not an advocate of that proposal."

COUNSEL: "And why is that?"

WITNESS: "World-famous physicist and mathematician, Stephen Hawking, once wrote something that struck such a chord with me that I memorized it.

"He said: 'We are such insignificant creatures on a minor planet of a very average star in the outer suburb of one of a hundred billion galaxies. So it is difficult to believe in a God that would care about us, or even notice our existence.'

"In the cosmic scheme of things, humans really matter very little. In my opinion, we need to learn our place in the big picture and not delude ourselves as to our own import. I believe humans would be best suited acknowledging our minimal role in the cosmos and focusing instead on matters we can actually affect. Famine. Global warming. War. Et cetera."

COUNSEL: "Thank you, Professor." Then to the Judge: "No further questions, Your Honor."

The Judge turned toward the opposite Counsel Table as its illumination increased.

JUDGE: "Cross examination, Counsel?"

The female attorney stood, facing the Judge.

COUNSEL FOR EXISTENCE: "Thank you, Your Honor."

She rounded her table on the far side and approached the center area near the Witness.

COUNSEL: "Thank you for coming here today."

WITNESS: "You're most welcome."

COUNSEL: "You have testified as to a good deal of what science says about the universe's past. Does science have anything to say about its future? I mean, where is nature heading with this unbelievably marvelous cosmos?"

WITNESS: "The Laws of Physics, specifically the Law of Entropy, predicts that the universe will continue to expand indefinitely. Many billions of years from now, the stars and galaxies will be widely dispersed throughout the universe. The night sky will be much less densely populated with celestial bodies. Of course, by this time, our sun will have burned out – maybe four or five billion years from now – and we will not be around to observe the state of the universe."

COUNSEL: "And what is the ending of the universe like? Does science hold any predictions for the final state of the cosmos?"

WITNESS: "Again according to the Law of Entropy, everything will continue to move farther apart from everything else. Galaxies will expand until gravity can no longer hold them together. Stars will burn out. Planets and asteroids will decay. Eventually, all that will be left will be a very thin fog of space dust, stretching to infinity."

COUNSEL: "Wow! It seems a long journey to nothingness."

WITNESS: "I suppose you could look at it that way. But as I have said, humans won't be around to observe the cosmic decay for very long. So the fate of the universe matters little to our species."

COUNSEL: "I see. Well let's move on to another area in which I have questions.

"I believe you have testified that subatomic physics can make a person's head spin. I confess that I am experiencing that effect right now. In order to help the Jury, I'd like to explore the theoretical underpinnings of these advanced scientific theories. Maybe that will help us put them in perspective.

"Are you willing to give it a shot?"

WITNESS: "Absolutely. What can I answer for you?"

COUNSEL: "At one point during your testimony, I heard you mention that gravity played a part in the formation of the cosmos. Can you tell us more about that?

WITNESS: "Certainly.

"The work of astronomers, physicists and cosmologists relies heavily on the predictability and constancy of gravitational forces throughout the universe. Without our knowledge of gravity, we could not explain why space dust and gases coalesce into stars, planets and asteroids. And we couldn't explain why galaxies, and even our own solar system, remain stable."

COUNSEL: "So I'm hearing that an understanding of gravity is pretty darn important in cosmology. Correct?"

WITNESS: "It's an absolute necessity."

COUNSEL: "So what is gravity, exactly?"

WITNESS: "Simply stated, gravity is the attractive force that exists between any two or more objects which have mass – in other words, objects that would weigh something on earth. Any objects with mass will be pulled toward each other by the gravity each possesses.

"A common example that we all can understand is that the earth's gravity pulls on the gravity of our bodies, keeping us from floating away, and making it hard for us to jump high or climb mountains.

"Does that answer your question?"

COUNSEL: "Partly. You have described what gravity does. But what *is* it?"

WITNESS: "That's actually a very astute question. Scientists are still not sure what gravity *is*. We know that gravity causes objects to attract each other. But we have not, thus far, been able to determine the nature of that attraction. It's not magnetic, as is the case with electrical fields. And it's not some external force pushing objects together.

"Yet it is clear that gravity exists. And the fact that its behavior is consistent is really all scientists need in order to use gravity as a predictor of actions in the universe."

COUNSEL: "Okay. Let's leave gravity alone for the moment. Is light also important to cosmology?"

WITNESS: "Definitely.

"The constant speed of light allows us to determine distances between the stars and galaxies. You have no doubt heard the term 'light year,' which is the distance light will travel in a year. A 'light year' is the standard unit for measuring distances across the cosmos.

"The speed of light is reflected in Einstein's Relativity Theory as the letter 'c.' Shifts in light wavelengths help determine whether celestial objects are moving toward or away from us. So light is definitely integral to our understanding of cosmology."

COUNSEL: "Can you explain to us what light is?"

WITNESS: "Most people refer to light as visible light. Visible light is a certain spectrum of electromagnetic radiation with a wavelength between 400 and 700 billionths of a meter.

"Scientifically speaking, the entire light spectrum includes radio waves at the low end, up to gamma rays at the high end. Radio waves can have a wavelength as long as several kilometers, while gamma rays may have a wavelength as tiny as an atomic nucleus. All could be considered 'light' in the scientific sense, since all consist of electromagnetic radiation, and all are parts of the same continuum of wavelengths."

COUNSEL: "Let's see if we can break this definition down a bit further.

"It's my understanding that waves travel through some medium. For example, if you throw a rock in the water, it makes waves that move up and down. The water doesn't actually travel forward with the wave. It just passes the rock's impact energy along to the water molecules next door.

"So for instance, if you are floating in a boat or an inner tube when a wave passes, you go up and down. You don't get carried along with the wave.

"Would you say that I have accurately described a typical wave, Professor?"

WITNESS: "Yes. But light is a bit more complicated."

COUNSEL: "I'm just getting to that, if you can bear with me for a moment."

WITNESS: "Certainly. Please proceed."

COUNSEL: "So typical waves transfer energy from one molecule to another through a medium – such as water or air – but do not actually carry the medium along with them as the energy is transmitted."

Counsel looked at the Witness for an affirmation.

WITNESS: "Correct."

COUNSEL: "But as you have said, light waves are 'a bit more complicated.' In fact, in many ways, light doesn't behave like a wave at all. True?"

WITNESS: "True."

COUNSEL: "In fact, light can travel through a completely empty space with no medium at all – including the vacuum of interstellar space. In such instances, it is not transmitting its energy *through* a medium. The light waves are actually projecting energy by moving the light *along with* the wave.

"Am I still on solid ground here, Professor?"

WITNESS: "I would agree with your statements. Yes."

COUNSEL: "So given this complicated behavior of light waves, can you explain to the Jury again exactly what light is?"

The Witness appeared to know where this was going. He shifted in his seat and briefly massaged his brow before answering.

WITNESS: "Perhaps I over-simplified my last definition. I'll try to give it another shot.

"It is true that in many respects light acts like a wave. It reflects off objects like waves do. It can also bend around objects as waves do.

"But in other respects, light acts like a stream of tiny particles – called photons – that are able to travel through a vacuum, as Counsel has already pointed out. A pure wave could not travel without a medium in which to transfer its energy. Light can. So it must be more than just a wave.

"Furthermore, scientists have measured the strength of photons of light emanating from the sun. The photons can actually push objects along with them as they travel through space. You may have heard of 'solar sails.' These are space-based, manmade structures designed to catch the 'solar wind,' if you will, to propel spacecraft through space. 'Solar wind' is just another name for the sun's electromagnetic radiation – its light.

"So sometimes light behaves like a wave. And other times it behaves more like a stream of particles – or a 'wind.'"

COUNSEL: "Thank you for your thoroughness, Professor.

"Let's move on to two other terms you have used in your testimony – 'nothing' and 'infinity.' I have some trouble understanding exactly what these terms mean in a cosmological sense.

"You have testified, if I recall correctly, that according to the Big Bang Theory, the universe began as a 'singularity' that was infinitely small and possessed almost infinite mass. And it appeared out of 'nothingness.' Did I recall that correctly?"

WITNESS: "Yes."

COUNSEL: "Can you give me an example of 'nothing'?"

The Witness wore a perplexed look.

WITNESS: "I'm not sure I understand what you're asking. Could you rephrase the question, please?"

COUNSEL: "Certainly.

"Is there an example . . . a single real world situation . . . in which nothingness exists? Or a single real-world thing that represents 'nothing'?"

The Witness contemplated the question.

WITNESS: "As far as we can tell, everything beyond our universe is nothingness."

COUNSEL: "Do you find that response very satisfying?"

WITNESS: "Not particularly. But the question is ridiculous. How can I point to something that is nothing? It's not possible."

COUNSEL: "But since you said the Big Bang Theory contemplates the universe arising out of something infinitely small and surrounded by nothingness, doesn't that make the theory an impossibility?"

WITNESS: "The Big Bang origin of the universe is not necessarily invalid just because we cannot currently duplicate the conditions that theoretically existed at the beginning of time. While it is true that I can't name something 'nothing,' and I would likewise fail to identify anything observably infinite, those deficiencies do not void the theory. Nothingness and infinity are clearly established as viable concepts in mathematics."

COUNSEL: "This cosmology sounds a lot like astrology to me. Philosophy and opinion masquerading in the guise of science."

Counsel angled her stance a bit more toward the Jury.

"You admit that gravity, light, nothingness and infinity are all crucial concepts to cosmology, yet you are at a loss to define even one of them. Your only excuse is that the field of mathematics, invented entirely from the minds of humans, allows for these things to exist.

"I'm sorry, Professor. I don't deny the usefulness of mathematics in explaining certain aspects of the physical world – things we can touch and see. But I can't grant theoretical mathematicians and astro-physicists *carte blanche* to invent the universe out of nonsensical, or ill-defined constructs.

"To be sure, it would be comfortable for me to say to myself: *These experts know the subject of which they speak, I should just take what they say as true, but beyond my comprehension. I needn't muddy the waters by requiring their theories to make common sense.*

"But I cannot – and will not – abdicate to another human being my personal responsibility to know my God."

She looked at the Jurors for a few seconds, then turned back toward the Witness.

"Thank you, Professor, for coming to speak today."

She turned to the Judge:

"No further questions, Your Honor."

She returned to her Counsel Table and sat.

COUNSEL FOR THE REPUDIATION: "Redirect, Your Honor."

JUDGE: "Please proceed, Counsel."

Counsel retook his questioning position.

COUNSEL: "Professor. Even if science does not yet know the precise means by which gravity exerts its pull, is gravity still a consistent and useful concept?"

WITNESS: "Yes. Of course. What we *do* know about the properties of gravity provides us with explanations for millions of observed phenomena – far too numerous to list."

COUNSEL: "And how about light? Is what we actually *do* know, and can objectively observe, about light useful?"

WITNESS: "If you are able to see me, you already know the answer. The lighting in this room is artificial. It is the properties of light we *do* understand that have allowed us to design artificial light sources . . . that is . . . light sources not found in nature. Again, the things we *do* know, and have already proven, concerning light are too many to recount here."

COUNSEL: "Would you say that the observations scientists have made of our physical universe are consistent with the properties we already know about gravity and light?"

WITNESS: "Universally so."

COUNSEL: "Is there any reason to suspect that observations that have not yet been made on the cosmic scale will contradict what we already know about light and gravity?"

WITNESS: "There is always a small possibility. But the chances are very, very, very, small."

COUNSEL: "Does it bother you that you are unable to point to examples of nothingness or infinity in the world around you?"

WITNESS: "Certainly not. These are concepts that defy human comprehension – yet clearly, they exist. Delving unendingly into the nature of their existence amounts to engaging in meaningless intellectual acrobatics. No further understanding will come of such endeavors."

COUNSEL: "Thank you again, Professor." Then to the Judge. "No further questions."

At this point the female attorney stood and addressed the Court.

COUNSEL FOR EXISTENCE: "Re-cross, Your Honor?"

JUDGE: "Proceed."

The woman remained behind her Counsel Table, bathed in the whiteness of the 'visible electromagnetic radiation' that we, apparently, weren't capable of understanding.

COUNSEL: "You mentioned that there are as many as ten spacial dimensions. Can you show me even one spacial dimension beyond the three we can all plainly see in this Courtroom?"

WITNESS: "No."

The Professor had given up playing her game. It was a good decision on his part.

COUNSEL: "No further questions."

After the Witness had been excused into the blackness, the Judge addressed everyone present. The standing attorneys were modestly lit, as was the Jury area. The artificial sky emanated a dusky blue/gold.

JUDGE: "The Jury will now retire to the Assembly Room for further deliberation."

"All rise."

We stood and watched as the odd Judge wheeled his way down the ramp and through the doorway toward his Chambers.

CHAPTER 15
THE FOURTH DELIBERATION

This time I found my designated seat quite quickly. I didn't even check to see who my table-mates would be. They would show up eventually.

Instead, I was wondering what time it was. We had turned our watches over to the Court Officer at about 9:45 this morning. By my estimation, it should have been time for a lunch break, or at least at rest room break, a long time ago. I unconsciously looked at my wrist.

Why wasn't I hungry or thirsty? And why hadn't anyone asked to be excused to use the wash rooms?

I stood as my Indian friend, Kimi, arrived. She was followed almost immediately by Tai and Dariah.

It was beginning to look like my deliberation group consisted of just six people – the four of us now present, plus Clete and Ariel. I thought it was wise that, at least for these intermediate discussions, our groups were small, and we were getting a chance to know the personalities involved. Trying to interact simultaneously with thirty-five strangers would have been extremely awkward.

We all shook hands . . . except Dariah, who bowed to each of us.

"Nice to see you all again," I said, when we were seated. "Where should we start?"

Tai jumped right in.

"I felt sorry for that poor cosmologist. The woman kept asking him such stupid questions. And he had to keep humoring her by trying to answer them. My blood pressure went up just listening."

Kimi and Dariah remained silent.

"I see your point, Tai," I said. "On the other hand, as I think the philosopher said earlier today, foolish assumptions lead to foolish results. It should be fair game to probe the basic understandings that underlie all the complex science that follows after."

Tai was about to say something. But I interrupted.

"Please hear me out. I'm not saying that we need to completely understand everything about an object, or a subject, for the knowledge we do possess to be useful to us. For instance, we don't need to understand how to build a car to drive one. Or know how a flower grows to enjoy a well-manicured garden.

"In fact, our understanding is incomplete in nearly every aspect of our lives, if you think about it. That doesn't keep us from living in a way that is consistent with what we *do* know."

Oh, God, I thought. *I'm starting to talk like an academic. I'd probably listened to too many of them today.*

"But to carry these analogies further, I wouldn't want to rely on a flower to produce seed for a turnip. Or expect my car to fly me to Singapore. So when we get to the point of considering extreme claims about things we only partly understand, having a good grasp of the fundamentals would be nice. Don't you think, Tai?"

"The cosmologist isn't exactly flying a Chevy to Honduras," Tai answered. "He's taking what he knows and making logical extensions of that knowledge."

"But that's exactly what I did with my car and my flower. I know the flower produces seeds and that turnips grow from seeds. I also know my car helps me get places fast. Planes do that, too. Why shouldn't I expect my car to fly? It's a logical extension of what I know to be true."

Tai was getting red in the face. I was doing the same thing to him that the female attorney had done to the cosmologist. This line of thought was certainly legitimate in my mind.

"But we *know* the car can't fly, and that turnips can't grow from flower seeds. We *know* that! It's not the same."

"I agree with you again, Tai. It seems silly for us to argue that a car can fly. We all have cars and no one has been able to make theirs fly. At least I'm pretty sure it would have made the news if someone had."

Everybody smiled at this absurdity. It helped lighten the atmosphere – even with Tai.

"But we *don't know* that the universe could have come from something infinitely small," I continued, "or that it was surrounded by nothingness. So there's all the more reason to question how we arrived at those conclusions."

Tai shook his head.

Kimi spoke up.

"Excuse me Mr. William and Mr. Tai. The things you speak of do not matter to me or to my beliefs. We do not ask Wakan Tanka to explain why the tree grows, or how the mountain lion learned to jump. The Great Spirit is in all living things, and that is enough for us – enough for me."

"And for me as well," Dariah added. "It may be something of western culture that requires you to have an answer to all things – to know all things. That is not my culture. Allah exists. I exist to bring praise to Allah. How Allah moves the stars in the heavens is a wonder . . . a divine mystery. I see the stars in the skies and praise Allah for his greatness."

Tai and I looked at each other. It was not going to be possible to debate Kimi or Dariah on their beliefs in the cosmological context.

"So Tai," I said finally, "aside from the issue of definitions that we have just talked about, what did you think of the rest of the Professor's testimony?"

"I know something of science, and I was most impressed with his knowledge of the cosmos. Of course, he could not relay to us everything that he knew, because it would take forever . . . and we probably wouldn't have been able to follow his lines of thought anyway. But as much as he spoke of . . . it seemed correct to me.

"That the universe is somewhere between 12 and 14 billion years old was predicted by Einstein's Relativity Theory nearly a hundred years ago. The Professor just fine-tuned that number based on the latest observations.

"I also believe, as I understood the Professor to say, that the universe began about 14 billion years ago in the Big Bang."

"Do you have unresolved questions about what *caused* the Big Bang, Tai? Or isn't that a problem for you?"

"Again, as the Professor said, the cause, if there was a cause, is subject to extreme speculation. Looking backward in time, all laws of physics would have ceased to exist once the spacial and time dimensions were gone.

"You could argue that a God started the Big Bang. On the other hand, you could also argue that it was some highly-advanced alien race from another dimension. Who knows?"

"So you believe that the Big Bang is a pretty well-established theory for how the universe began?"

"Yes. Certainly the vast majority of scientists accept it."

"May we discuss the first man's evidence – the man who said there is no God?" Dariah asked.

"Sure," Tai said. "Go ahead."

"I am troubled by what this man has seen, because I, too, have observed it to be true. People who go to Mosque regularly, pray frequently and speak of piety and love . . . their actions very often do not match their words. This may be true even for the Imams – our religious leaders. They preach of peace and praise for Allah, yet gather together armies to kill other Muslims. I do not know how to understand this . . . this . . . confusion."

I could tell that Dariah had been troubled by this question before today.

"In my experience," I said, "it is very common for people to get turned off to religion because they believe religious people should lead model lives. In fact, all major religions teach that it is not possible for humans to lead perfectly obedient and loving lives. So why do the non-church-goers expect perfection? I think there are a couple of reasons.

"When people abuse or criticize or mistreat others, claiming that their religion tells them to do this, these people are not followers of their religion. No mainstream religion teaches these things. Such people are like the tyrants who make pretexts for their tyranny. They would do the same things and lay the blame elsewhere if putting off their behavior on religion were not so convenient – and effective. The answer for dealing with all of these people is to recognize that they are not what they claim to be. They are not religious. Then there is no inconsistency between their claimed religion and their actions.

"The second group is more difficult to explain. These are people who go to church, or mosque, or synagogue, or wherever, and really *believe* what their religion teaches. But they lack the conviction to *trust* their beliefs in their daily lives.

"For example, many religions teach that God will provide His people with everything they need, no matter what happens. Yet the believers don't trust God on this issue. They hoard their possessions, and perhaps even steal property from others, to make themselves confident that they will be provided for. They trust themselves more than they trust their God. So their behavior conflicts with their words."

"Okay," Tai said. "I'll buy the first group. They're just bad folks who do bad things and blame it on religion. I know they're out there.

"But the second group . . . I'm not so convinced. How can you really *believe* something and then not *act* on it. It's like believing the sun will rise tomorrow, but recharging all your flashlight batteries tonight – just in case. Seems like a stretch for the word 'believe.'"

"If I may speak Mr. Tai and Mr. William and Ms. Dariah," Kimi said. "Among my people it is a common belief that all creatures know what is right to do. But all creatures sometimes choose to do that which is wrong, even in their own eyes. It is because creatures are not perfect. Only the Great Spirit is perfect.

"The man with no God who spoke today . . . he said the same

things. He believes it is wrong to cheat and steal, yet he does so when it suits him. So it is for all creatures – perhaps for man, most of all."

Suddenly, I surprised myself by remembering the substance of a particular sermon I'd heard preached many years ago. *Where had that come from?*

"In Christianity," I recited from the sermon, "we call doing those things that we know to be against our beliefs – that we know to be wrong – sins. We believe it is in our nature to sin. Only with God's help can we hope to improve our behavior. In that sense, our churches are much more like hospitals for sinners, than they are museums for saints. No one can truly measure up to the standard of a sinless life."

"Still, when our religious leaders sin, or commit *khati'a* as we say in Islam," Dariah added, "it is worst of all. When *they* sin, the world sees all people of our religion as sinners. It is wrong. But it is."

"Okay," Tai added. "I'll grant you that religion doesn't have the market cornered on bad dudes. Maybe judging a religion, or a God, based on people's behavior is not such a good idea."

"And yet, Mr. Tai, the believer should still judge herself on her own actions."

"As should the atheist," was Tai's response.

At this point, the discussion ended. The Court Officer had appeared to fetch us to the Courtroom once more.

CHAPTER 16
THE SECOND COSMOLOGIST

When we entered the Courtroom and filed to our new seats, the Courtroom lighting had returned to its normal level – the fully lit room with the three-dimensional blue sky ceiling and faux windows we had seen upon our first visit here.

I found myself looking around more closely at the walls, floor, ceiling, even the chairs in which we were to sit. For a good part of this trial it had seemed as though most of the Courtroom didn't actually exist. Such was the illusion presented by the finely contained, and sparely applied, lighting which had visually dominated the proceedings thus far.

I sat in my assigned seat like the obedient Juror I had become. The bizarre illumination, the unnerving appearances and disappearances of Witnesses, the impressive theatrical effects, and the total absence of a time reference, combined to give the Courtroom an eerie, apocalyptic feeling.

The blend of lighting-dominated staging, with the heady lectures of the academics, and the heart-rending testimonials of the two beleaguered women, left one afloat somewhere between intellectuality and emotion. The sensation was truly unique – and I suppose – oddly appropriate, for a trial of God's existence.

The two attorneys emerged from the Chambers doorway and headed for their Counsel Tables. I prepared to stand up.

"All rise."

We rose.

"Hear ye! Hear ye! This Court is now in session. The Honorable Judge Jonathon Cole presiding."

After Judge Cole had resumed his seat in the leather lift-chair, he said: "Please be seated.

"Ladies and Gentlemen of the Jury.

"Counsel for the Repudiation of God has informed the Court that he will be presenting no further Witnesses at this time. Therefore, we will proceed with the opposition Witnesses."

He turned toward the female attorney.

JUDGE: "Please call your first Witness."

The room went black – at least nearly black. After my eyes adjusted, I could see the Judge's Bench glowing its soft, golden hue, and Counsel for Existence was gradually coming into focus as she approached a still-dark Witness Stand. By the time she had reached her questioning position, her light was fully white, and a wholly-lit, middle-aged Caucasian man had appeared on the Stand.

The Witness was slender, but comparatively broad-shouldered, with a well-muscled neck. He wore a cream-colored, long-sleeved broadcloth shirt, open at the collar. His eyes held a sparkle . . . a glint of passion. For what, I couldn't tell.

COUNSEL FOR EXISTENCE: "Please state your name for the court and then fill us in on your professional credentials."

WITNESS: "My name is [indistinguishable]. I hold a Bachelor of Science in Physics from the University of Michigan and both a Masters of Science and a PhD in Astronomy from the University of California at Los Angeles. I have also done research as a postdoctoral fellow at UCLA in the area of quasars and galaxies. I currently work as a research astronomer for NASA and teach astronomy part-time at the Wiess School of Natural Sciences at St. John's University."

His accent was Canadian, but not prominently so.

COUNSEL: "Thank you, Doctor.

"Since it seems you have spent a good deal of your life's focus exploring stellar phenomena as an astronomer, I am wondering to what degree you are familiar with the field of cosmology?"

The Witness smiled broadly.

WITNESS: "I believe that nearly every astronomer who takes more than a passing interest in his or her vocation eventually becomes a cosmologist. You simply can't keep making amazing observation after amazing observation without beginning to wonder what is behind it all.

"So, yes. I have a great deal of familiarity with cosmology."

His body language was animated. His voice, alive with energy.

COUNSEL: "You have heard the testimony of Professor [indistinguishable] regarding his knowledge of cosmology – is that correct?"

WITNESS: "Yes. I listened in with interest."

COUNSEL: "Do you have any observations about the Professor's testimony and its accuracy or inaccuracy?"

WITNESS: "Yes. I can say that I generally concur with the Professor's outline of the theories of the universe, and with his timeline for the development of life on earth. Of course, he could not possibly say all there is to say about cosmology. And I would probably have focused on some different aspects of the cosmos than did the Professor. But as far as they went, his facts were correct and well-articulated."

COUNSEL: "You know that this trial is about whether God exists. Yes?"

WITNESS: "Of course. I was informed."

COUNSEL: "Could you direct our attention to aspects of the cosmos that you believe warrant further elucidation – a different 'focus' as you say – in light of our trial goals?"

WITNESS: "It would be my great pleasure."

COUNSEL: "Please enlighten us."

WITNESS: "First of all, although I have already said that I agree with the last Witness's facts and theories, I could not disagree more with his conclusions – particularly about God's role in the cosmos. I see God's fingerprints upon every aspect of the universe . . . from the very beginning forward.

"As you have already heard, the Big Bang postulates that the universe arose from an infinitely small object with nearly infinite mass and energy. To say that something is infinitely small is the same as saying that it has no existence at all. Even mathematical equations treat infinitely small numbers as being equal to zero. So when the universe burst forth from this infinitely small dot, this singularity, for all intents and purposes, it appeared from nothingness.

"Before I go further, I need to acknowledge one point that you raised in your cross-examination of the Professor. It really isn't possible to make any logical sense of something that is 'nothing' or 'nothingness.' And for that matter, our brains cannot comprehend anything that is 'infinite' or that had no beginning.

"I am not saying that mathematical or physics theories that make use of these concepts are without merit. But it *is entirely reasonable* to question their foundations. I am glad you did so.

"On the other hand, one also needs to recognize the limitations of the human mind. It is certainly possible for something to exist that humans could never make sense of. 'Nothing' and 'infinity' might be two of those things. God is another. So we need to be open to such concepts.

"Getting back to the Big Bang . . . I believe, although I cannot prove, that there was a cause for the Big Bang. To argue that there was no cause at all because there was no time dimension in existence is a leap significantly beyond established physics. If a cosmologist is willing to throw out one of the most fundamental tenets of physical science, Newton's Law of Causation, one has to question whether there are ulterior motives at work. I shall discuss this idea more in a moment.

"Since our universe – *the* universe – came into existence out of nothing, I am also convinced that the cause of the Big Bang came from some dimension, or from some reality, outside of our universe itself. My rationale is again one of causation. In order for something to 'cause' itself to exist, that something would have to already 'exist' in the first place. So the argument is circular. Something *outside* of the universe had to cause it to come into existence.

"Are you following my line of thought here?"

Counsel looked to the faintly lit Jury Box for an indication of understanding. As I looked around me, I could see modest acknowledgments of comprehension. But nobody's head was exactly bobbing up and down with exuberance.

Counsel returned her attention to the Witness.

COUNSEL: "I think we're okay. Please proceed."

WITNESS: "If one accepts that there was a cause for the universe, one must logically ask what that cause might be. At this point, all science is out the window. Everything a scientist knows, everything that can be proven, comes from within our universe. There is no scientific basis for extending the principles we have observed here to a spacial dimension, or another universe, beyond our own. So the cause of the universe is reduced to a guess, an assumption, a desired result, or a faith.

"The other lawyer fellow over here," he motioned toward the Repudiation Counsel's Table, "compared God to an invisible fairy. It sounds laughable. But if one has nothing at all to go on, why couldn't this gentleman's fairy have created the universe?"

There was subdued laughter from the Jury Box.

"No, really. If there are no scientific indications regarding causation, what might make one particular cause of the universe any more likely than another? It's a fantastic question actually. And it's one I asked myself a number of years ago as an undergraduate at the University of Michigan.

"At the time, I was young, smart and confident of my abilities. And justifiably so. I had been a brilliant success at every intellectual pursuit I had undertaken in my short life. And I made the same mistake that many of us make when we are very good at something. We assume that we are very good at everything – or at least many things.

"In any case, I was confident enough to *know* that I had no need of a God in my life. My wits would guide me. I didn't require supernatural solutions to questions in my world or my studies. I would find answers on my own.

"In short, I was a cocky little S.O.B."

A more robust round of laughter erupted from the Jury Box.

I thought of Tai.

"So when I came up against this issue of the beginning of the universe, I first tried to prove its cause. Obviously, for the reasons I have already explained, my efforts resulted in abject failure.

"Once I had discovered that science and wits were not going to allow me to prove the true cause of the universe, I was determined to at least put to rest any folderol to the effect that its creation was the work of some God – some figment of the weak-minded masses.

"At first, I struggled with how to disprove God. Then I fell upon the idea that if God were truly present in some religious doctrine, evidence of his existence should be clearly set forth in the Holy Book of that religion. There should be proof that the words of the book were inspired by a Being with knowledge beyond that which its writers could have possibly possessed.

"I was confident that my investigation would find no such evidence of God. And then I could put the 'God myth' on the same level as the 'invisible fairy' in competing for creation honors. There would be no reason to prefer a God over an alien race, or an inexplicable 'singularity.'

"I embarked on what would turn out to be a multi-year quest to disprove God. During the course of the journey, I not only read, but studied and researched, every Holy Book of every major religion on earth. Judeo-Christianity, Islam, Buddhism and Hinduism were the big four. But I researched several tribal religions and Native American belief systems as well.

"For the first several years, my thesis remained intact. I had not come across a Holy Book that revealed any Godlike insights into the universe.

"Then I came to the Bible.

"As I read the opening verses of the Book of Genesis, I could literally feel my eyes widen. In just the first few hundred words, the author of the Bible had described all of the major cosmic processes, from the Big Bang to the dawn of humans.

"Furthermore, they were all in precisely the correct order!

"According to the Bible, God first created light and darkness – the earliest observable effects of the Big Bang. Then he created the earth. Initially, it was 'formless and empty' – an accurate description of the earth's early development from a collection of space rocks, to a molten sphere, and finally to a round, dry, lifeless rock.

"Genesis goes on to recount the evolution of earth's atmosphere – 'sky' – and the separation of land and water that eventually developed as the planet cooled. This was followed by the creation of plants, then sea creatures, then birds, and finally, land animals.

"The last creature to be made was man.

"I was astonished. How could a writer who lived thousands of years ago possibly know the order in which the universe, our planet and its living inhabitants, had evolved? Scientists were making many such discoveries during just the last century or two.

"But I certainly wasn't going to be derailed from my thesis by a few hundred, admittedly symbolic, words at the beginning of the Bible. I would search this book carefully to find its contradictions – to discover where its message diverged from scientific fact.

"I was eighteen months in the process of studying the Bible. Somewhere between when I started and when I finished, I became a Christian.

"Although I cannot recount to you all of the Biblical references that bore out modern scientific truths, I can give a few examples.

"Cosmology describes the universe as arising from a singularity in the midst of nothingness and then continually expanding – stretching outward and displacing the nothingness all around it. To be clear, the Big Bang was more than just stars and galaxies shooting out into 'space' that was already there. In the beginning, there was no 'space' as we know it . . . only 'nothingness' – no spacial dimensions at all. No up. No down. No sideways. No time.

"There's a big difference.

"When we say the universe is expanding, we mean the very fabric of space itself – the area occupied by the three observable spacial dimensions – is stretching out, taking the celestial bodies and the area between them with it.

"The idea that the universe is expanding is a twentieth century phenomenon. So in the Bible when Isaiah says that the Lord 'created the heavens and stretched them out,' this was a concept that could not possibly have been perceived by Isaiah. He would have observed a static universe – stars in fixed celestial positions. He would have no reason to believe that the universe had been 'stretched out,' or would continue to be 'stretched out.' Yet this same reference to God 'stretching out' the heavens appears in twelve separate Bible verses, authored by five different writers.

"Another example of Biblical precognition is a verse in the New Testament Book of Hebrews where the writer states: 'By faith we understand that the universe was formed at God's command, so that what is seen was not made out of what was visible.'

"Wow! This author has just described a transcendent God – one who makes things in our universe from things that were not previously here. Similar statements recur in multiple Biblical passages.

"Of all the Holy Books, only the Christian Bible accurately, repeatedly and consistently describes the universe in ways that could not have been observed by the writers. The only source had to be a Being who knew how creation had occurred.

"God!

"It is truly amazing how my attempt to disprove God resulted in my accepting Him into my life.

"But this was only the beginning of my awareness of God in the universe. With new knowledge of the cosmos pouring in over the past several decades, I have begun to see more and more evidence that God is at work. And that humans are truly His chosen species."

The Witness paused for a moment . . . probably to allow some of what he had just said to sink in.

COUNSEL: "So you say that your reading of the Bible has led you to the conclusion that God *must* have inspired its writings? That there is *no possible way* the authors of the Bible could have observed, or otherwise known of, the details of the creation and the universe's expansion as described in that book?"

WITNESS: "That is precisely correct.

"When I have a lot to say, I sometimes tend to get ahead of myself. I'm pleased that my point is clear."

COUNSEL: "I believe you stated that you had found other evidence, outside the Bible's correlations with scientific fact, that led you to believe God was the Creator – the cause – of the universe. Would you elucidate, please?"

The Witness had literally worked up a sweat during his last monologue. He had to take a fresh breath before proceeding.

By this point it seemed clear to me that his passion was for his religion. He reveled in sharing his beliefs.

WITNESS: "It would be my pleasure.

"Many of the Jurors have, by now, heard of the theory of the universe called Intelligent Design. The same theory is also referred to as the Anthropic Principle. The theory of Intelligent Design is not so much a scientific theory as it is an observation of scientific facts and their probabilities.

"It is a well-established scientific fact that human life cannot exist unless many independent characteristics of our universe are all true. The theory states that the probability of all of these characteristics being true in a randomly created universe is so infinitesimal, that our universe must have been specifically designed for the purpose of allowing human life to exist.

"As recently as 1960, scientists believed that the universe might hold millions, or even billions, of earthlike planets that could sustain human life. This initial assumption was based on an 'inhabitable planet' requiring just two characteristics – the right kind of star, and the right distance from it.

"Basing his estimates on just these two requirements, astronomer Carl Sagan estimated that approximately .001% of all stars in the universe could have a planet capable of supporting human life. Multiplying this probability by the approximately 100 billion stars in the Milky Way, Sagan concluded that there might well be more than a million earthlike planets in our galaxy alone.

"Since the early sixties, the list of requirements for a habitable planet has grown longer and longer. For example, we now know that any habitable planet must have the right gravitational pull to allow it to retain in its atmosphere certain crucial gases like oxygen – atomic weight 18 – while shedding excess quantities of poisonous ammonia – atomic weight 17 – and methane – atomic weight 16. If the earth's gravitational force was off by as little as a few percent, the planet would either be suffocating in ammonia, or seriously short on oxygen.

"In addition, the rotational period of the planet would have to be just right. If it were too slow by more than a few percent, the temperature differences between day and night would be too extreme for life. If it were to spin too fast, wind velocities would be unbearable. Jupiter's rotation period is just ten hours. Even a calm day on Jupiter features winds of more than a thousand miles per hour.

"A satisfactory planet must also contain the right amounts of essential minerals, such as arsenic, cobalt, iron, oxygen, fluorine and numerous others. Many of these elements essential for life are also deadly to humans if their quantities are too great. Requiring that inhabitable planets possess the necessary quantities of all of these crucial elements, without exceeding their toxic levels, would eliminate all planets except one in every 10^{26} planets. 10^{26} is a 1 followed by 26 zeros.

"When more complex factors – such as atmospheric density, inclination of a planet's orbit, rate of deuterium production in the universe, the location of a planet's star relative to such interstellar hazards as supernovas, black holes and binary white dwarf stars – are taken into account, the probability that life could happen by chance on earth becomes impossibly small. So small that we cannot even imagine it.

"One scientist has analogized the chances of even one planet in the universe being capable of sustaining life as follows: 'Cover a billion land masses the size of the United States with stacks of dimes reaching to the moon. Then ask a blind person to pick out the single red dime from the huge collection on the very first try. The chance of any planet in the universe being capable of supporting human life is much worse than that blind man's chance of finding the red dime on his first pick.'

"Unimaginable!

"And the more observations scientists are able to make, the more 'incredible coincidences' they find. One astronomer has calculated – he believes conservatively – that the chances of an earthlike planet capable of sustaining life coming into existence anywhere in our universe purely by random acts of nature is in the vicinity of one planet in every 10^{166}. When you know that there are estimated to be a maximum of 10^{22} planets in all of the universe, you see how truly 'miraculous' earth really is."

The Witness pulled a note card out of his shirt pocket and examined it briefly.

"A self-proclaimed agnostic, Robert Jastrow, may have summed it up best as he watched his colleagues measuring the cosmos."

The Witness now read from the note card.

"Jastrow once wrote:

'For the scientist who has lived by his faith in the power of reason, the story ends like a bad dream. He has scaled the mountains of ignorance; he is about to conquer the highest peak; as he pulls himself over the final rock, he is greeted by a band of theologians who have been sitting there for centuries.'

"I could go on in more detail about nuclear forces that need to be in balance, and cosmological constants that must be fine-tuned, but it is all redundant and points to the same conclusion. The cosmos is no accident.

"The universe, in all its power and splendor, was designed especially to support human life here on planet earth.

"Before I leave this subject of Intelligent Design, I must repeat to you the quintessential metaphor supporting this theory. Although the same story has been around for more than four hundred years, its present incarnation is attributed to British Philosopher, William Haley. A paraphrase of Haley's version, updated to contemporary century word usage, goes like this:"

At this point the Doctor referred to a second note card he had been holding. He held the card out and began a dramatic recitation, employing a slight British accent.

"'In crossing a heath, suppose I struck my foot against a stone. Then someone asked me how the stone came to be in that place. I might possibly answer, that for all I knew, it had lain there forever. And not many would disagree with me.

'But suppose instead of the rock, I had found a watch on the ground, and someone was to inquire how the watch happened to be there. I can't imagine giving the same answer as I had for the stone – that it had probably always been there. It would be obvious that some craftsman, some skilled watchmaker, had designed and constructed the watch for the purpose of telling time – that the watch had not come about by chance.

'Every indication of planning, every manifestation of design, which existed in the watch, exists in the works of nature. The only difference is that, in nature, the level of complexity is much greater – greater by a degree which exceeds all computation.'"

The Witness lowered his note card and spoke directly to the Jury.

"The watch is the universe. God is the watchmaker supreme. His purpose in making the universe is to foster and support the human species. Chance alone cannot explain our existence. God's influence is evident everywhere we turn."

He turned his attention back to Counsel.

"Is there anything further I can answer for you, Madam?"

His voice retained a hint of the British accent as he spoke.

COUNSEL: "To be perfectly clear, you propose that the earth could never have existed in its present form without divine intervention. And there is ample evidence in recent scientific observation to support the notion that the universe was designed – and not just designed, designed exquisitely. Designed for mankind.

"Am I hearing you correctly?"

WITNESS: "In spades.

"But one doesn't need a particle accelerator, or a space-based telescope, to look around at the earth, the sun and the stars and to know that something truly miraculous is going on – that some Being of great power has created the universe and allowed us to live in it.

"That is, unless, one chooses not to see."

COUNSEL: "Thank you, Doctor, for your insights and information." Then to the Judge: "No more questions for this Witness."

As she returned to her table, Counsel for Repudiation readied himself for his cross-examination.

JUDGE: "Do you wish to cross-examine this Witness, Counsel?"

COUNSEL FOR REPUDIATION: "Yes. Thank you, Your Honor."

He brought a yellow notepad with him to his usual examining spot – near the Witness, facing forty-five degrees to the Jury.

COUNSEL: "Doctor. Would you agree that the whole Big Bang Theory still has its dissenters? I mean, it's not a unanimously held theory. It is possible that there never was a beginning and that the universe always has just existed?"

WITNESS: "Yes. I mean it is certainly possible that the universe has always existed and there was never a beginning. Some scientists still advocate that position – though not many.

"But then, the Flat Earth Society still has members who maintain, despite all evidence to the contrary, that the earth is flat and surrounded by a forty-five-foot-high wall of ice."

The Witness smiled politely.

There were chuckles from the Jury.

COUNSEL: "I see you have a sense of humor. I like a good sense of humor. "

WITNESS: "And I as well."

COUNSEL: "But your answer to my question was that it is, indeed, possible that the Big Bang Theory is incorrect, and that the universe has, in fact, existed forever. True?"

WITNESS: "Yes. That is a possibility."

COUNSEL: "Are you familiar with the word 'Anthropomorphism'?"

WITNESS: "Yes."

COUNSEL: "Could you describe for us your understanding of what 'anthropomorphism' is?"

WITNESS: "Surely.

"Anthropomorphism is the tendency of humans to attribute human qualities or attributes to something that isn't really human at all. In the context of cosmology, it is more narrowly concerned with humans blinding themselves to any evidence which does not support the idea that the universe was created just for them."

COUNSEL: "Well put. Much better than the definition I had here in my notes."

WITNESS: "Thank you."

COUNSEL: "Do you agree that many humans exhibit anthropomorphic inclinations?"

WITNESS: "All the time. People think their dogs are psychologically distressed, or their cats love them, or their lawn mower is obstinate."

COUNSEL: "In regard to cosmology, how does anthropomorphism manifest itself?"

WITNESS: "Those who are opponents of Intelligent Design claim that scientists who believe in the Anthropic Principle only look for evidence that supports their theory that the universe is built for man and man alone. So naturally, that is all the evidence they find. They don't find the contradictions."

COUNSEL: "Isn't it also true that some scientists and philosophers attribute evidence of Intelligent Design to human self-centeredness and ego? In other words, we look around, and we are such self-absorbed creatures that we can't imagine that all we see isn't made just for us? And furthermore, we believe we are such lovable creatures that we assume there is a God who loves us and gives each of us His attention 24/7?

"Would you agree that those arguments have frequently been made in opposition to Intelligent Design?"

WITNESS: "Yes.

"In fact, one of the more clever metaphors places humans in the place of a flea on a dog's back. The flea looks around and very logically assumes that this dog is such a perfect home and provider for him, that the dog must have been created solely to fulfill his needs."

COUNSEL: "Once again, very well put."

WITNESS: "Of course, the flea has a rude awakening when the dog gets a flea collar. But I suppose that is neither here nor there."

Again there was laughter from the Jury.

COUNSEL: "And the arrival of that flea collar would be analogous to earth being hit by a large asteroid, of the variety that caused the extinction of the dinosaurs and 90 percent of all life forms on earth.

"We humans are but a cosmic stone's throw from annihilation, so to speak."

WITNESS: "If we are, indeed, wiped out by such an asteroid, I will concede the point. However, that last big collision with a space rock was sixty-five million years ago. We may have a bit of a wait."

The Jurors were clearly enjoying the verbal banter.

COUNSEL: "Getting back to the idea that too much effort is going into finding reasons why humans are central to the purpose of the universe . . . if we are, indeed, so blinded by our own aspirations, what evidence disproving Intelligent Design might we be missing?"

WITNESS: "We could be missing all sorts of evidence. We

wouldn't know for sure until we found it."

COUNSEL: "So you concede that there may be evidence in the cosmos – perhaps even very substantial evidence – that would contradict the Anthropic Principle? That would deny man his import?"

WITNESS: "Of course. That's the thing about science . . . everything's possible until someone proves it isn't. But I must point out that there are a good many scientists searching eagerly for just such evidence. It has not yet been found."

COUNSEL: "Let's switch topics for a moment. Returning to your discussion of how you came to the Christian faith by reading the Bible . . . I've looked at some of the Bible passages to which you refer, and they don't seem to have cosmic ramifications to me. In fact, some of them seem to be directly contradictory to science.

"For instance, the Bible says the world was created in six days. Science says that it took 13.7 billion years. Wouldn't you say that's a discrepancy?"

WITNESS: "You could say that. Or you could take the biblical language as being figurative or metaphorical. After all, how would God explain to an ancient human that there actually was no day or night for nearly 10 billion years?

"And what details could God give to the primitive human mind to explain the fusing of elements, the interaction of celestial bodies, the effects of cosmic radiation. These people thought that simple illness was caused by a curse or a demon. Even Jesus, himself, spoke in parables to make complex situations relevant to his audience.

"After reading many ancient texts, I had already learned to think metaphorically. In a metaphorical context, the Bible is smack on!"

COUNSEL: "Isn't there some danger that we're getting involved in a Nostradamus situation here? The man made some obscure predictions, and his followers have been bending them as much as necessary to fit actual events. It's rather like fortune telling. Predict a future event in broad enough terms and almost everyone will find that future event somewhere in their life?

"'You will meet a handsome stranger. Your luck will change for the better. Work hard and your efforts will be rewarded. I see a large sum of money influencing your destiny.'

"Seriously, Doctor. Don't the words of the Bible simply amount to soothsaying? Broad guesses at how the world might have formed?"

WITNESS: "Not in my opinion.

"If you refuse to be convinced of these things, I cannot convince you. I learned that bit of wisdom long ago. But the Jurors . . . they will have a chance to look with their minds open. They will either choose to see, or not to see. They will discern the truth, or reject it. All I can do is keep answering your questions."

COUNSEL: "Yes. Well. Very interesting philosophy. But not at all helpful to finding God at the beginning of all things."

WITNESS: "To me it is."

COUNSEL: "No more questions for this Witness."

He returned to his table as the light grew on the female attorney.

COUNSEL FOR EXISTENCE: "No further questions, Your Honor."

JUDGE: "The Witness may be excused."

The Witness's light blinked out.

CHAPTER 17
THE MINISTER

JUDGE: "Counsel, please call your next Witness."

COUNSEL: "The Witness is ready, Your Honor."

JUDGE: "Please proceed."

The female attorney approached the Witness Stand where the next Witness 'appeared as if from nothingness,' just like the universe itself.

I wondered why we couldn't drop the technical gimmicks by this point in the trial. Honestly, they were getting on my nerves. A few tricks at the beginning. A hidden projection system. Some dramatic lighting effects. The combination *did* create a mood. But it was getting old now and I wished it would stop.

COUNSEL FOR EXISTENCE: "Please state your name and relevant professional credentials."

He looked to be a fellow of Scandinavian descent. Reddish-blond hair. Round face. Light complexion. He was wearing his work attire – black shirt and pants with a white preacher's collar. I assumed he was a minister of some sort.

WITNESS: "My name is [indistinguishable]."

Damn it! I was sick and tired of not hearing the names. Why should anyone want to hide their names? Why were they always inaudible?

WITNESS: "I hold a Masters of Divinity from Luther Theological Seminary. I am currently serving as Head Pastor of a Lutheran congregation of about 3,000 members."

COUNSEL: "Reverend. Could you please tell us how you came to your Christian faith?"

WITNESS: "People ask me that a lot. I'm afraid I haven't come up with a simple answer. For me, it was sort of a process.

"My dad was a pastor. That meant we moved around a few times while I was growing up. He pretty much went to minister wherever the Synod called him to serve. And his family went along.

"Being a PK, a pastor's kid, is a sort of unique experience. On one hand, you certainly get a healthy dose of religion in nearly every aspect of your life. On the other, it's sort of hard to think of your dad's workplace as some place 'holy.'

"My brother and I used to run all through the church while we waited for Dad to finish writing a sermon, or counseling a parishioner, or doing whatever else he did to hold those congregations together. When our friends would come to church on Sunday all whispering and nervous, my brother and I were just hanging out like usual. It's a feeling most people never experience.

"After graduating high school and heading off to college, I guess you could say that I had a weak spell in my faith. I seldom went to chapel services at school, opting instead to sleep in late. I can't recall religious encounters of any significance during those early college years – except one occasion when I came home for a visit and tried to sleep through a Thanksgiving morning church service."

He smiled at the Jury. My impression was simply that he was a nice guy in a weird outfit. More normal than I had expected from a front-line man of the cloth.

"Toward the end of my junior year I met a young woman who would later become my wife. When I first saw her, she was playing guitar and singing Judy Collins songs at the campus coffeehouse. Her singing voice was lovely. And the rest of her was pretty nice, too."

The Jurors laughed openly.

"I spent that whole night sitting alone at a small table near the stage, trying to work up the nerve to ask her to sit with me at a break.

As it turned out, I didn't have to ask at all. During the intermission between her last two sets of music, she disappeared behind the curtain and slipped out the stage exit. Before I knew it, she was pulling out a chair and joining me at my table.

"Perhaps my enraptured posture was a bit obvious."

There were laughs from the Jury Box.

WITNESS: "Here I was, all worried about asking her, and she was bold enough to approach me without my even saying a word. I guess you could say she had faith.

"She was a regular attendee at campus chapel services and active in the campus ministry. So it wasn't long before I became involved in those activities as well. Seeing religion through her eyes brought to me a whole different perspective from my PK upbringing. Suddenly, I had a personal relationship with God – at first through my girlfriend, and then gradually, through my own journey of faith.

"After graduation, we decided to marry young. I went to the seminary while she worked retail jobs to pay the rent. And the rest, as they say, is history."

COUNSEL: "So there was no instant of recognition – no flash of lightning – that made you a Christian?"

WITNESS: "Not that I recall. As I said, it was sort of a process, with its ebbs and flows. Of course, that may not be the case for others. Every believer has his or her own faith experience."

COUNSEL: "What exactly do you mean by 'faith experience'?"

WITNESS: "The process by which a person comes to believe in God . . . to have faith."

COUNSEL: "Faith sounds like it's going to be the watchword of your testimony. Why don't you tell us the role that faith plays in a Christian's belief in God."

WITNESS: "The questions certainly don't get any easier as we go, do they," he said, mostly to the Jury.

Again there was light laughter.

"Christians understand that we can only believe in God through faith. And faith is not of our own doing, but by the free gift of God.

How one comes to have faith is, to me at least, a mystery. Contrary to popular belief, it is not a pastor's job to instill faith. Rather, it is his mission to minister God's word to all who will listen. If a nonbeliever hears God's word, and is open to accepting it, God will give that person faith."

COUNSEL: "Would you mind giving us an example of how someone you know came to faith? Maybe a 'typical' faith experience?"

WITNESS: "I don't know if there is such a thing as a faith experience that's 'typical.' But here's one example.

"At one time, there was a man in my congregation who died in a dreadful car accident at the age of forty-five. He left surviving a wife and two adult sons, ages eighteen and twenty. Funeral arrangements were held at our church. The service was widely attended.

"After the service was over, many of the attendees chose to stay for a sandwich and a visit with family members of the deceased in the church fellowship hall. Before the meal, I said table grace, then stood against a wall, watching. Folks began working their way along the folding-table buffet of turkey sandwiches, potato salad and mixed nuts.

"The immediate family members went through the serving line first. As they filled their paper plates, I noticed that the younger son walked with his mother and brother, but didn't take any food for himself. When the other two took their plates and coffee cups to a table to eat, the younger son, Alex, headed in my direction. I watched as he maneuvered between the white-clothed tables – head down, hands at his sides.

"When he reached me, he looked up and I saw that he was crying.

"'Alex, would you like to talk to me?' I asked him.

"He nodded his head.

"'C'mon.' I motioned for him to follow me to my office down the hall.

"We each sat in one of my upholstered side chairs and I asked how I could help.

"'How come God let Dad die?' The words came with sobs. 'I hate

God!'

"I reached out my hand to Alex's shoulder and prayed silently that God would inspire my words to this grieving young man.

"'I can't tell you why your father died,' I said. 'But I *can* tell you that God is here now. And he was with your father when he died. The Bible says, 'I am with you always – even unto the ends of the earth.' So I know God was with your dad, and He gave your father comfort after the accident – just as He is here, willing to comfort you, if you will let Him.'

"Alex began to weep uncontrollably. I sat with him, neither of us speaking. Gradually, he regained some measure of composure.

"'Alex,' I said. 'Do you know where your father is now?'

"'In heaven . . . with God and the angels,' he whispered through sobs.

"'Then you don't need to cry for him, do you. You can certainly cry for your loss and for how you will miss him in your life. But don't cry alone. Let God into your heart to help you with the pain. Now is when you need God the most. Don't shut Him out.'

"'I'll try.' he said. But Alex continued crying.

"We sat together for a while longer.

"'Would it be all right if I said a prayer for you and your family?' I offered.

"Alex nodded his assent.

"I said a short prayer with Alex. Then he wanted to be alone. I let him use my office as long as he wanted. I saw him later that day. He was still very sad. I wondered if I had said anything at all to be of help.

"On a Sunday about twelve years after his father's death, Alex was visiting our congregation with his wife and young daughter. He greeted me warmly. Then he asked if we could talk privately.

"We found a quiet spot.

"'I just wanted to tell you, Reverend, how you changed my life the day we buried my father.'

"I was surprised to hear he even remembered our talk, let alone considered it a life-changing event.

"'Before Dad's death, I wasn't much of a Christian. I mainly went to church to please my folks.

'But after you left your office that day of the funeral, I prayed to God for comfort. I felt like I had fallen into an abyss and there was no way out. God answered my prayer. I didn't hear His voice, or see a vision, or anything like that. But when I finished praying, I knew we would be all right.

'I haven't stopped talking to God since.'

"I knew that I hadn't said anything particularly inspirational to Alex. God allowed my words to open Alex's heart to faith. Faith was God's gift to Alex – not mine.

"That was the beginning of Alex's faith story. I can't say where it will lead him, or how the story will end. But the day his father died, Alex accepted God's free gift of faith, and it has forever changed his life journey."

I couldn't help but see the parallel between Dad's minister asking to pray with me, and the story I had just heard. *Had I made the wrong choice in shunning the preacher's offer? How could it possibly have mattered?*

The Reverend paused a moment. I could tell that this had been an emotional story for him to tell. He looked up at Counsel.

WITNESS: "Will that example suit your needs?"

COUNSEL: "Yes. Very much so. Thank you for sharing Alex's story with us.

"I do have one more question, though. I understand you to say that God comes to everyone in different ways, under varying circumstances. Is there anything that these circumstances have in common? Any universal pathway to faith?"

WITNESS: "I can't say that I have ever understood a universal pathway to faith. In fact, faith remains, to me, very much a mystery. Yet it also seems to me that two elements are probably necessary for one to receive faith.

"The first requirement is that the person must hear of God's existence and his relevance to the person's life. Such sharing of the word may be in the form of a sermon, a conversation, a written note, an email, a text message, by the reading of the Bible – any form of communication at all.

"Second, the person needs to open their mind to the possibility that God exists, and that God wants a real relationship with them. If a person's mind is closed to God, and he refuses to accept faith, that person will never attain it. That is why I minister God's word to as many people as possible. If only some of them will open their hearts and minds to Him, God may inspire them to faith through my words – unworthy as those words may be."

COUNSEL: "Thank you for your time, Reverend." Then to the Judge, "No further questions for this Witness, Your Honor."

Counsel for Existence returned to her table while Counsel for Repudiation prepared to begin his cross-examination.

COUNSEL FOR REPUDIATION: "Reverend. You spoke often of 'faith' in your testimony. What is faith to you?"

WITNESS: "The Bible says that 'Faith is the assurance of things hoped for – the conviction of things not seen.' I don't think I have a better definition."

COUNSEL: "I'm still a little unclear how someone gets faith. Can you, as an ordained minister, impart faith to a willing mind?"

WITNESS: "No. I can express my faith. And I can offer counsel. But faith must ultimately come from God – not from my words or actions."

COUNSEL: "Then how does someone who does not have faith come by it?"

WITNESS: "Only God knows exactly how a person's faith is ignited. But reading the Bible with an open mind, and asking God to give you faith, might be a good start."

COUNSEL: "It sounds like I would have to be pretty desperate to open a book and pray to its author to be my God. Why not open the refrigerator and pray to KitchenAid to be my God?"

There was open laughter in the Jury box.

COUNSEL: "I'm sorry, Reverend. I don't mean to be flippant. But what would lead me to think that I could find God in the Bible, as opposed to in the writings of Shakespeare, or Thoreau?"

WITNESS: "As I have said, I am not fully knowledgeable about how God imparts faith. I don't believe any human completely understands. It is what we call a 'Divine Mystery.'"

COUNSEL: "Let's look at this a different way. Do you have faith that, if I tried to kill you right now, God would save your life?"

WITNESS: "My life? I don't know. My soul? Yes. Absolutely."

COUNSEL: "Wouldn't faith be a whole lot easier to come by if God made a clear demonstration of His presence? Why not more miracles? A more prominent display?"

WITNESS: "First, I will answer your question about miracles and faith. I believe that, because of the free will God has bestowed upon man, there is no miracle God could perform that would give a closed-minded person faith. Whatever act God displayed, no matter how magnificent and mysterious, a person who chose not to believe would see only trickery, magic, or perhaps some demonstration beyond their knowledge. That person might actually choose to believe in your fairy over God. It is their free will to do so.

"Second, it is difficult for me to imagine God having a more prominent presence in the lives of mankind than He already displays. Step outside. See the sun burning fiercely the perfect distance from earth so we are warmed and plants can grow. Breathe the unseen air, without which we could not live. Marvel at the hills God has raised up through forces powerful beyond human comprehension. Speak the language your miraculous brain has acquired. Then tell me God is not here."

COUNSEL: "I can appreciate your belief that these wonderful coincidences are God's doing. But science can explain them all. So pardon me if I don't need to believe that 'only God can make a tree.' Men graft them all the time – and grow them from seed. Regularly. Predictably. Scientifically."

WITNESS: "Yes. What a remarkable mind God has given man!

Isn't it wonderful that God has provided scientists with so many mysteries to explore that they shall never satisfy their thirst for knowledge. There will always be more unknowns to be revealed.

"Who knows? Maybe one day man will even be able to *make* a seed . . . not just plant one. But that knowledge will make seeds no less miraculous."

COUNSEL: "It seems to me, Reverend, that in order to get faith, one must already possess it. Since God is impossible without faith, He cannot exist."

WITNESS: "Your statement is incorrect. It is faith that is not possible without God – not the other way around."

COUNSEL: "It is clear, Reverend, that we shall forever remain at odds over this faith issue. Do you agree?"

WITNESS: "Unless you open your mind to God, of your own free will, I suppose that is so."

COUNSEL: "No further questions for this Witness.

The Witness was excused in the usual fashion. The Jury adjourned for further deliberation.

CHAPTER 18
THE FIFTH DELIBERATION

My discussion group this time consisted of Ariel, Clete and Kimi. We still hadn't taken a break for lunch. But no one seemed to notice.

"That first guy," Ariel began, "the cosmetologist. He seemed like a really smart guy. And if he's right that the chances of there being a planet like earth anywhere are like a bzillion to one, somebody must have made it special. It couldn't just happen. There would have to be a God.

"Right?"

Clete had an observation.

"Ariel, honey, Mark Twain used to say that there are three kinds of lies – lies, damn lies and statistics. What that cosmologist was spouting was statistics. I don't really know if I can believe any of it. There's so much voodoo science behind all that stuff, that there's no way to know if what he was sayin' is truth, or just made up speculation, backed up by statistics that he pulled out of his backside. You might get some other expert up there that uses the same statistics to prove just the opposite. Or he might have a whole new set of facts and figures to befuddle and amaze."

I was witnessing our discussion as it drifted away from logical analysis and thought I should chip in.

"You know, both of you guys are right . . . up to a point. When people don't understand where the statistics come from, they have the sound of something factual and proven.

"My reading of Twain says that statistics are bad because sometimes people use them to deceive. I don't think he would've meant for us to throw out the mathematical science of statistics for appropriate purposes.

"On the other hand, we can't just accept numerical odds at face value either. All those extremely low probabilities were the results of simply multiplying the estimated chances of individual planetary characteristics occurring in nature. If some, or nearly all, of these characteristics were interdependent, the math might be all wrong."

"I don't get what your sayin'," Clete said.

"Me neither." It was Ariel. Her eyes had glazed over when Clete mentioned statistics.

Kimi remained silent.

"Let me see if I can explain more clearly.

"The most popular team sport in the world is soccer. Right?"

Everyone nodded.

"So let's say that I'm watching a team sport, but I can't see it well enough to determine which sport it is. I know that sounds a little weird. But please bear with me.

"I'm going to determine the probability that the team sport I'm watching might be soccer. I have a set of statistics to help me calculate the probability. And I'm going to apply them strictly – in a mathematical way – to find the chances that I'm watching a soccer game.

"Here are the statistics – which I have made up for purposes of this example:
- 50% of all team sport games I might be watching at any given place in the world and at any given time would be soccer games.
- 70% of all team sports involve the use of a ball.
- 60% of all team sports involve the use of a *round* ball.
- 2% of all team sports involve a time clock that doesn't stop running at all during the game.
- 1% of all team sports involve most players using their feet,

but not their hands.

"Now if I multiply all of these probabilities together to determine if I am watching a soccer match, I would multiply the 50% chance that the game would be soccer, times the 70% chance that the game would involve a ball, times the 60% chance that the game would involve a *round* ball, times the 2% chance that the game is one in which the clock never stops running, times the 1% chance that the players are using predominantly their feet.

"Let me jot all this down and do the math for a second please."

I wrote the numbers down and multiplied them out.

"The result of all this multiplication is that the probability that I am watching a soccer game is .0042%. Of course, that probability is nonsense. If half of all the team sports matches going on in the world at any given place and at any given time are soccer games, it should be pretty much a 50/50 chance that my game is a soccer match.

"Although all of my statistics were true requirements of a soccer match, they were redundant. So I shouldn't have multiplied them at all. They were already encompassed in the 50% figure I started with."

Clete was still pondering. Ariel appeared totally at sea.

"How does this apply to the cosmologist's statistics?" I continued. "Well, we can assume that he knows what he's talking about and that the statistics he multiplied are truly independent statistics.

"Or we can assume that they are a meaningless conglomeration of mathematical manipulations, aimed at proving a specific point – namely, that the odds of our earth being inhabitable by humans without God's intervention are impossibly small.

"Whether his statistics are useful to us in our deliberation depends entirely on whether you trust the cosmologist's competence and his honesty. Or whether you believe either quality may be in question.

"Of course, you need to judge those things for yourself."

Ariel sighed dramatically.

"I was hoping it would be easier than that."

"Lies, damn lies and statistics," Clete repeated.

Kimi had been listening to everything intently, but had not offered her opinion.

"Kimi," I asked, "do you have any thoughts you'd like to share?"

"Mr. William. Once again, the things of which you are speaking mean little to my beliefs. I understand what has been said. But is it not foolish for me to ask what the chances are that you, or Mr. Clete, or Miss Ariel exists, when my eyes see you before me and my ears can hear your voices?"

The rest of us at the table sat staring at Kimi. I, for one, had no rebuttal to her position. I wondered if she really could see God – or if she had been culturally brainwashed into thinking so.

Kimi's unswerving belief in her God was both inspirational and unnerving. It seemed that, by this time in my life, I should have a solid belief in *something* about God. But the more evidence I heard, the more willing I was to consider the options.

Was my intellect interfering with inspiration? Or *vice versa*? I suddenly felt unqualified to sit as a Juror in this case. My thoughts were divided. I was no longer sure that reason alone was the path I should follow.

"Okay . . . ," said Clete. "How 'bout we talk about the minister."

"Sure," I said. "What have you got to say?"

"Well, he weren't like none of the ministers I know back home. Where's the hellfire and damnation? Now *there's* a reason to believe in God!

"This faith stuff he was spoutin' seemed kinda . . . I'm not sure what's the right word here . . . fuzzy? I mean, I know ya gotta have faith to be a believer. But that's just mostly goin' to church and sayin' your prayers and stuff."

Ariel had been waiting for her chance on this issue.

"My daddy says I got faith when I was baptized and I'm going to heaven for sure, no matter what. Because of Jesus and the cross and stuff. So I got faith all right. I go to church, say my prayers, even read the Bible sometimes. And I try not to be mean to people. When I get married, it's gonna be a church wedding and God will be there to bless our rings.

"So all that talk about faith . . . well . . . I know I got it. I can't give it to anyone else. So I guess I'm set."

Ariel seemed to have resolved her faith issues. Kimi spoke next.

"It is not the Indian way to force our spiritual beliefs on others. So that, I will not do. But I will share them with you.

"My belief . . . my truth . . . my 'faith' is mine from my father and my mother, and from their ancestors before them. It is passed from generation to generation. So it has always been. So it will always be. It does not spring forth from the mind or from the heart. It is part of us.

"The Reverend seems to me a kind man, and a man devoted to his beliefs. But of his faith, I cannot make comment, for his faith is strange to me."

It was my turn.

"I liked the Reverend as well. He seemed pretty down to earth for a preacher. And I have to say that the story about the boy who found faith at his father's funeral was quite moving. But no matter how much he explained faith, and how you get faith, I couldn't help feeling that something was missing – some logical link was absent.

"I felt like the male Counsel. How do you choose to believe one thing and not another? Put differently . . . how do you choose one *faith* and not another? Or for that matter, none at all?

"If faith is indeed a 'mystery,' as the Reverend says, I wonder why that is so? Why is the ability to believe in God a mysterious process? Shouldn't everyone have free access?

"I have a vague sense that faith stems from a relationship, like a family. Relationships take time to mature . . . time for trust to develop. But how do we get that relationship started with God? I don't know.

"I'm sorry. I have only questions on this topic. No answers."

"Well," Clete summarized, "it sounds like when it comes to faith, Kimi and Ariel say they've got it. And you and I are still confused.

"That about right?"

"That's about it," I said as Kimi and Ariel nodded.

CHAPTER 19
THE PSYCHOLOGIST

Once the Judge was back on the Bench and we had all been seated, the lighting changed again as Counsel for the Existence of God began questioning her next Witness.

This Witness was another Caucasian man, probably in his fifties. His attire consisted of a brown suit, cream-colored shirt and tan tie, with brown shoes and socks. His thick, salt-and-pepper hair looked like he'd spent too much time in front of the mirror.

COUNSEL: "Please state your name and list your professional credentials for the Court."

WITNESS: "My name is [indistinguishable]. I earned a Bachelor of Arts in Human Interactions from Hampshire College and a Masters Degree and PhD in Psychology from Columbia. My specialty is in cognitive behavioral psychology. I am presently a Clinical Psychologist practicing in the Mental Health Clinic at Johns Hopkins University."

COUNSEL: "Could you please describe for the Jury what a Clinical Psychologist does?"

WITNESS: "Yes. A Clinical Psychologist is a medical professional who works to help alleviate his patients' mental suffering or mental disorders, and to promote their general mental well-being.

"The primary tool of the Clinical Psychologist is counseling. We meet with patients who are exhibiting behavioral or cognitive abnormalities and seek to aid the patient in relieving his or her condition.

"I should probably note that psychology must be distinguished from psychiatry, which has similar goals for helping patients to address mental issues. The psychiatrist is a medical doctor and primarily treats patients with medications – not counseling."

COUNSEL: "Thank you, Doctor."

WITNESS: "You're welcome."

COUNSEL: "Now Doctor, as a Clinical Psychologist, are you familiar with the term 'egotism'?"

WITNESS: "Yes. 'Egotism,' also called 'Egoism,' in its extreme form, is the tendency to place oneself at the center of one's existence, having little or no concern for others, or for the world in general.

"The pure Egoist would only take actions that he or she believed would accrue to his or her own benefit – either immediately, or in the long run. Even apparently selfless actions, such as giving time or money to charities, would be seen as motivated by the Egoist's desire to feel generous.

"There aren't too many psychologists around these days who would tell you that pure egoism is the primary motivator for man's actions – although it is common knowledge in the profession that most humans, given the opportunity, will usually act in their own self-interest instead of in the interests of others.

"Of course, exceptions exist. But even the most altruistic individual will occasionally act in ways that tend to favor his own interests, or exalt his own importance or status, over those of others."

COUNSEL: "So are you saying that a certain amount of selfishness is sort of built into the human psyche?"

WITNESS: "A certain amount, yes."

COUNSEL: "Can you give us examples of egoistic manifestations in what you would consider a 'normal' personality?"

WITNESS: "Certainly. Let us say that Bloomingdale's has a big sale. People will crowd around the doorway, anxious to be the first into the store. They may even run over or push others to get what they want, though under most circumstances, they would never consider such behavior.

"Or a person may hold onto a certain belief against all evidence to the contrary, simply because they perceive a change in that belief as a threat to their societal stature or their self-image. An example might be a police officer who knows down deep that he is homosexual. He can't admit this fact, even to himself, let alone his comrades, because of the macho culture of the police department.

"If he admits his innate sexual leanings, he knows his micro-culture will consider him weak and unmanly. This is true even though it is well-established that sexual orientation has no effect on bravery, loyalty or any other character trait that police hold dear."

COUNSEL: "So if I understand you correctly, you're saying that normal people will often act in their own self-interest, just because it is part of their natural makeup to do so?"

WITNESS: "Yes. That is correct."

COUNSEL: "You have heard the testimony given in this trial. Yes?"

WITNESS: "Yes."

COUNSEL: "Can you tell us whether the human tendency to act selfishly, or to exalt – I believe that was your word – oneself above others, has any bearing on scientific observations of God's involvement at the beginning of the universe?"

WITNESS: "Yes. I can see where egoism might come into play in several ways."

COUNSEL: "Please elaborate."

WITNESS: "I will certainly do my best.

"From the testimony presented thus far, I understand that the conditions existing at the moment the universe came into existence cannot scientifically be proven. So any theory of origin must reach beyond the realms of the provable and into the venue of belief.

"For a scientist, who has placed his faith in the testability of the scientific method, and in his own intellectual ability to figure things out for himself, egoism would tend to push him in the direction of a belief that the origin of the universe is explainable and rational.

"He has no need for a supernatural explanation. In fact, he may even find the idea that a God created the universe repugnant. If there is a God who created the universe, and who can manipulate its properties from time to time, then the scientist's proofs of natural laws, chemical properties and physical interactions would be relegated to second position behind God's ultimate set of rules. A scientist may not embrace the demotion.

"Another interesting thought is that the self-centeredness present to some degree in all human minds might cause us to consider any God to be a threat to humanity's supremacy in the universe.

"Think about it. If there is no God, who or what would be the greatest, most intelligent, most advanced being in the universe? Humans. So if a person has no convincing evidence one way or the other, his self-centeredness would lead him to conclude that there is no God – thus ratifying his own supremacy."

COUNSEL: "So if the human tendency for self-centeredness tips the scales in favor of humans as supreme being, should humans be skeptical – or at least cautious – before throwing out the God hypothesis?"

WITNESS: "Absolutely. We really should acknowledge our own biases in favor of ourselves and ask the God question thusly: 'Can I prove God *does not* exist?' To ask whether God *does exist*, actually puts God at a disadvantage when humanity is the judge, because of God's competition for the title of 'supreme being.'

"Do you follow me?"

COUNSEL: "I believe you are saying any jury of humans would have some tendency to be disposed to reject God, because God threatens their status at the top of nature's pyramid. And that fact, in and of itself, makes them biased against God."

WITNESS: "Exactly. To be fair to the possibility of God, we need to negate our own self-interest by placing the burden of proving God's *nonexistence* on ourselves – not requiring God to prove that He is out there."

COUNSEL: "You have raised some interesting considerations,

Doctor. Thank you for your time today.

WITNESS: "It has been my pleasure."

COUNSEL: "No further questions for this Witness, Your Honor."

COUNSEL FOR THE REPUDIATION: "Cross, Your Honor?"

JUDGE: "Please proceed."

Counsel for the Repudiation moved slowly toward the Witness – a cat ready to pounce. I could think of many angles from which to attack this Witness. I wondered which he would choose.

COUNSEL: "So humans have a tendency toward self-centeredness."

WITNESS: "A tendency. Yes."

COUNSEL: "And an inclination to, perhaps, overinflate their importance in the cosmic scheme."

WITNESS: "Yes. I should think so."

COUNSEL: "If a human believed that mankind was the primary reason for the entire cosmos to exist, that would be an example of humans overinflating their importance. Wouldn't it?"

WITNESS: "If the human has no rational basis for that belief, yes. I would say it would be such an example."

COUNSEL: "And what, in your view, would constitute a rational basis for humans to believe that they are the center of cosmic purpose?"

WITNESS: "Evidence such as was presented a while ago by the cosmologist. Evidence that a planet appropriate for human life is extremely unlikely to exist by mere chance as a result of natural processes alone."

COUNSEL: "But Doctor, isn't it true that you, yourself, have a predisposition in viewing evidence of God's existence? Isn't it true that you are a believer in the Christian faith? And that as such, your belief in God would more than compensate for your innate selfishness when it comes to weighing such matters as evidence of God's existence?

"Isn't that correct, Doctor?"

The Witness took a few seconds to consider the question.

WITNESS: "I'm not sure how one would determine the relative weight to be given to each bias."

COUNSEL: "I suppose not."

The last was delivered with no small amount of sarcasm.

COUNSEL: "No further questions for this Witness."

Counsel returned to the dimness of his Counsel Table and his light went out.

CHAPTER 20
TESTIMONIALS FOR GOD

Again, the Jurors sat in near total darkness – the only lighting in the room being the ever-present glow of the Judge and his Bench.

"At this time," the Judge announced, as the light surrounding him increased in intensity, "we will hear Testimonials from Witnesses who have had experiences that led them to belief in God, or strengthened their faith. As with the previous Testimonials, Counsel will not be asking questions of the Witnesses.

"Please give your full attention to the Witnesses as they speak. Do not expect further clarification from the attorneys."

The Judge turned in the direction of Counsel for the Existence of God, whose light now shined dimly.

"Counsel. Please produce your Witnesses."

At once the Judge's light diminished to its usual level, while Counsel for Existence remained faintly lit.

THE THIRD TESTIMONIAL

Counsel for Existence took her seat, disappearing from view as a brightly lit black man appeared in the center of the area between Jurors and Judge.

He was slender – perhaps six feet tall, maybe 165 pounds. His short-cropped hair framed a face that spoke of a hard life. Among pock marks and scars was a particularly prominent slash across his right cheek. He wore a brown business suit, white shirt and a colorful tie with an unusually large knot.

"My name is Paki," he began in a strong voice.

His accent was an African version of British. He spoke somewhat haltingly.

"I was born in a small village approximately 100 kilometers distant to the south from Addis Ababa in Ethiopia. I am twenty-seven years old."

His visage was that of a man many years older.

"I have three brothers and two sisters . . . though I am not sure that they are still living. I have not spoken to them, or heard from them, in nearly twenty years.

"When I was a small boy, my family was very poor. We lived in a one-room hut built from rocks and mud. The roof was made of grass. The government allowed us a small parcel of land to feed ourselves. But we had no oxen or goats for milk. And our few chickens could not lay enough eggs to feed all of us. The land itself was poor. Though we toiled endlessly, it would not produce enough grain to make the flour for our flat bread.

"My family was a good Catholic family. My mother taught me the love of Jesus and the compassion of God. Even as a young boy, I knew that God was always with me.

"One day, not long after my seventh birthday, my father sent me to our village to trade eggs for milk. It was my first trip to the market alone.

"While I was there, bad men with rifles raided the village, stealing produce and livestock from the market, and capturing many young men, women and children, of which I was one. The men bound their captives together with hemp and made us to walk in a line, alongside the oxen and goats, many miles to The Sudan.

"There I was sold for money as a slave to a wealthy farmer and herdsman. The man's name was Chimola.

"With my hands bound in rough rope, Chimola brought me to his farm. Chimola rode his camel while I walked, or was dragged, behind.

"When we arrived at his property, Chimola tied me to a post in the farmyard. His children taunted me, calling me '*abeed*,' which means 'Negro slave.' They beat me with sticks until I was bloody and could not stand."

His eyes looked upward, as though recalling the pain.

"After Chimola's children had finished beating me, and he saw that I could endure no more, Chimola sent me to sleep in the barn with the oxen and his other slaves. There, the slave women saw to my wounds and did their best to comfort me.

"The next morning, Chimola had me brought to his house. He changed my name to 'Chakide,' which in English means 'weasel.' He also told me that I would now be Muslim and the other slaves would teach me about Allah.

For ten years, I lived as Chimola's slave. At first, being a mere boy of seven years, I worked with the women around the house and barn. I swept floors, fed chickens and learned to mend clothing. As I grew older, Chimola trusted me to help tend his livestock, plant his crops and bring them home from harvest. For the most part, I was treated decently. But I had no freedom.

"Each day during all this time, I prayed to Jesus and his Father in heaven to deliver me from Chimola. I also prayed that, while I remained in Chimola's keeping, my burdens would not be too great for me to bear.

"Twice, when I was fourteen years of age, I ran away from Chimola. The first time, I had been alone tending the herds and began to run north along the dirt road.

"I did not know where I was going. I just ran. But after several miles, Chimola's men found me and brought me back to the farm. There Chimola beat me with a leather whip. This scar on my face is from that beating."

He pointed to the slash on his right cheek.

"Chimola told me that if I tried to escape him again, he would kill me.

"Two days later, I ran off once more – this time in the other direction, through the woods. Again, Chimola's people found me and brought me back to him.

"Chimola was furious with me and meant to shoot me with his hand gun. I prayed that God would save my life. As Chimola went to the house to get his gun, I heard Chimola and his wife talking.

'Do not kill him,' she begged. 'He is too valuable to us. It would cost us much to purchase and train another to perform his duties. Instead, beat him once more and let him be.'

"God turned Chimola's heart. All I received as punishment was a beating with a wooden cane. No more was said of killing me. But Chimola made me promise to never try to run away again.

"That was a promise I knew I could not keep forever.

"Three years later, when I was seventeen years of age, I ran from Chimola for the last time. I escaped to the village market and hid among the crowds. There I found a Muslim man who did not believe that slavery was just. He owned a truck. And he agreed to take me north, beyond Chimola's reach. I hid in the back of his truck as we left the market, and Chimola's farm, behind forever.

"I had escaped Chimola. But now I had nowhere to go.

"When we arrived at the man's village, God opened the man's heart. He gave me food and drink. He even bought me a bus ticket to Khartoum with his own money, for I had none. In Khartoum, he told me, there was a group of people from my own tribe, living as refugees.

"From Khartoum, my new friends in the refugee camp obtained for me a false passport and arranged passage for me to Cairo. My hope was to reach the Catholic Church of the Sacred Heart – a place that was well-known among my tribesmen for helping people such as myself.

"Through God's mercy, I made it across the border into Egypt and to the church without great difficulty.

"I remained at Sacred Heart for several months, studying the English language, in hopes of obtaining refuge in the United States. But the journey was yet to be a long one.

"As soon as I was able to find employment, I left Sacred Heart to live in an apartment nearby. I continued to pray and to study.

"Finally, after many months, I was granted United Nations refugee status. I was now free to go to the United States, if only someone would sponsor me. By God's grace, it was mere days after the United Nations approved my status that I received a notice. An American church organization had agreed to sponsor my escape to the United States. They would provide me with food, western clothing and a home until I could make my own living.

"Try to imagine the picture, if you will, when nineteen-year-old Paki walked off the airplane onto the runway in Fargo, North Dakota – in January."

There were small laughs from the Jury.

"I was not certain that living in this cold would not be worse than on Chimola's farm. But of course, I was given appropriate clothing and shelter . . . and I met many new friends.

"Best of all, I had freedom.

"It was truly a blessing to be living in Fargo those first months. With my new friends' help, I had found a job. I could not imagine a better life. God had been very generous to me. I wanted for nothing, and gave God great thanks for the goodness and mercy He had shown me.

"Then one day, a man in a suit knocked on my apartment door. He said he was from a United States Senator's office. He wanted me to speak to Congress about slavery!

"I was frightened beyond my wits at the man's request and asked for several days to consider it. As you can hear, my English is not good. It was even worse at that time. I was very afraid to speak in English before many people.

"After hours in prayer, I believed that God wanted me to go to Washington to tell my story. I hoped that, if word of my life was heard in the United States – the most powerful country in the world – someone here could do something to help stop slavery and torture in my homeland. God had chosen me to be his instrument in this way.

"Today, I have come a long way baby."

The Jurors laughed at Paki's joke.

"I am proud to say that I am the only living slave to shake the hand of a United States President. I travel endlessly, speaking to anyone who will listen of the need to abolish slavery in all the world. I speak also of how God rescued me so I am able to tell my story.

"I know in my deepest heart, that God was with me through all my life. When I was enslaved, he gave me hope for freedom. When I was beaten, I knew that he would heal me. When I suffered delays on my journey, he gave me patience and the will to persist. And when I reached the United States, he gave me a voice much louder than any I deserved of my own right – not to raise myself above others, but to bring freedom to those in bondage, and glory to Him who gave me words to speak of their plight.

"To God, I give great thanks. I give praise to His glory. By His strength, and not by my own, I have lived my life in faith. And I trust Him in all things."

Paki raised his right hand in benediction.

"May God's peace be with you and His face shine upon you all."

Then Paki clasped his hands at his waist, gave a small bow to the Jury, and his light went out.

THE FOURTH TESTIMONIAL

The lights had only been out for a few seconds when a new scene was revealed before us. This one was another multi-media presentation of some sort.

Spread out across the open space appeared a hospital delivery room. A very pregnant woman wearing a hospital gown was reclining on the bed, her knees raised and covered by a powder blue cotton blanket.

A man leaned over one side of the bed, holding her hand in both of his. A woman doctor and two assistants wore surgical drapes over blue hospital uniforms and stood in the foreground. They held their rubber-gloved hands up and away from their bodies.

The scene was a frozen vignette. No one moved and no one spoke. There was no beeping from the monitors that we could see wired to the woman's abdomen.

Then the woman raised herself on her arms, revealing perspiration-drenched blond hair and a face red with exertion. She inhaled deeply, as if to catch her breath. Everything and everyone else remained frozen.

"My name is Elise," she said, as she breathed again. "This is my husband, Brian." She looked in the direction of the man by her side.

"We have been trying to have children for the past ten years. Not much more than a year ago, we gave up on fertility treatments. We were resigned to remain childless. It was a relief, actually, to put an end to the guilt I had felt for not being able to give Brian a child.

"During that whole ten years, we had prayed and prayed for God to give us a baby. I conceived more than once. Each time, the pregnancy ended in miscarriage. With every lost child came mourning and grief . . . and more guilt.

"Rationally, I knew that I was not in control of my reproductive system. And I had followed every recommendation from the doctors. Diet. Exercise. Vitamins. I didn't smoke cigarettes or drink alcohol. And I have never used drugs.

"Even so, the guilt persisted. I felt responsible for my barrenness.

"After grieving the loss of our last child to miscarriage, Brian and I decided that enough was enough. It was not going to happen for us. We thanked God for comforting us through our ordeals, and asked Him to help us to be okay with our new, childless, future.

"Three months later, I was pregnant with twins.

"At first, we were very guarded about our optimism. We had been down this road before. We knew all too well the tragedy that might lie at the end. But we have continued to pray that, this time, God will let these babies live.

"We're in the delivery room now and I'm fully dilated. Say a prayer for me that all goes well."

Now everything was in full motion. The monitor beeped erratically. Brian was holding Elise's hand tightly saying "You can do it, Honey. Just a few more minutes."

The doctor had lifted the blanket and sheet from Elise's legs and was in position to begin the delivery.

DOCTOR: "The first baby is crowning, Elise. With the next contraction, I need you to push as hard as you can. Can you do that Elise?"

Elise was physically spent from her labor . . . her breathing like that of a distance runner nearing the end of a long race. With each breath she seemed to be running shorter on oxygen. She gasped for air.

ELISE: "I don't know if I can . . . . I'm so tired!"

BRIAN: "You can do it, Honey. Just a couple more minutes and our babies will be here. You can do it."

Elise's body began to tense up.

DOCTOR: "Okay, Elise. Here comes the contraction. Push hard. Push Elise."

Elise groaned as she pressed every ounce of her being into delivering the baby.

DOCTOR: "That's it Elise. The baby's head is out. Here comes the rest. I've got her Elise. A baby girl."

BRIAN: "Oh, Honey. A baby girl! You're doing great! Just a little while longer. You can do it."

The doctor handed the infant to the operating room staff person, who proceeded to clear the baby's airway and dry her off. Momentarily, the infant let out a healthy bawl. The staff person wrapped her in a small blanket and examined her closely, noting, I assumed, her Apgar Score – the standard measure of a newborn's health.

The doctor remained busy at the delivery table.

STAFF MEMBER: "First Apgar is 9. Very good, Elise. A very healthy little girl. Good job, Mom."

DOCTOR: "Okay, Elise. Try to rest between contractions. Consciously relax your muscles. I'm going to palpate for the second baby's position."

Elise tried to relax as the doctor examined her birth canal.

ELISE: "Another contraction is coming. Should I push?"

DOCTOR: "Try not to push with this contraction, Elise. I want to assess the baby's exact orientation. Its head is not crowning yet."

ELISE: "Oh God! It feels like I need to push!"

BRIAN: "Remember to breathe. Deep breaths. In and out. In and out. You can do it."

ELISE: "I've got to push, Doctor. I can't help it."

DOCTOR: "Try not to push, Elise. Do your best."

I couldn't tell if Elise was pushing or not. But she was focused and straining as hard as she could to deliver the second child. Her arm and leg muscles quivered from exhaustion.

DOCTOR: "The umbilical cord is wrapped around the baby's neck, Elise. You've got to try your very hardest *not* to push."

The doctor's words were not scolding or panicky. But they conveyed clear urgency.

The contraction subsided and Elise lay back on the delivery table, thoroughly drained and trying hard to catch her breath.

STAFF MEMBER: "Fetal heart rate is at 70, Doctor."

BRIAN: "What does that mean, Doctor?"

The doctor was trying to maneuver either the fetus or the cord using her fingers inside Elise's birth canal.

DOCTOR: "I'm busy right now. I'll explain later."

ELISE: "Here comes another contraction."

DOCTOR: "Don't push. Try hard not to push."

STAFF MEMBER: "Fetal heart rate is at 60 and falling."

DOCTOR: "Page a pediatrician, stat. Try not to push, Elise."

The staff member picked up a wall phone and spoke to someone.

ELISE: "I can't help it! I can't help it . . . . I have to push."

The doctor reached out toward one of the staff without removing her attention from the delivery.

DOCTOR: "Umbilical scissors."

The staff member selected the tool from a nearby tray and slapped the scissors into the doctor's outstretched palm. I could see the doctor make a quick cut with the scissors in the area where the delivery was taking place. The doctor tossed the scissors onto a steel pan attached to the table.

DOCTOR: "Okay, Elise. Push! Push hard!"

ELISE: "I'm pushing as hard as I can, but the contraction is over. I'm trying."

BRIAN: "You can do it, Elise."

STAFF MEMBER: "Fetal heart rate at 50."

DOCTOR: "We need to get this baby out now! Push as hard as you can, Elise."

Elise appeared about to pass out. Brian was now supporting her back to aid the delivery.

DOCTOR: "Okay. Good, Elise. The baby is out. Another girl. Try to relax now."

A staff member accepted the baby from the doctor, moving it rapidly to a clear plastic enclosure. The doctor stayed with Elise.

DOCTOR: "100 percent oxygen," she said to the staff person, without taking her eyes off Elise."

At this point, I could see that Elise was bleeding from between her legs. Blood ran off the delivery table and onto the floor.

DOCTOR: "Elongated forceps. One unit of O-Positive, IV Push."

A different staff member slapped the requested instrument into the doctor's palm, then moved to hang the bag of blood on Elise's IV pole. A few moments later, the doctor delivered the placenta onto the table-side tray.

Elise slumped into unconsciousness. Brian laid her flat on her back.

Another doctor had arrived in the delivery room. He hastened to join the staff person tending to the baby in the plastic box. He was leaning over it, doing something rhythmic with his arms and hands. Resuscitation?

Both doctors were working feverishly on their failing patients when the scene froze once again.

This time it was Brian who spoke.

"Elise had lost a lot of blood having the babies. A long hard labor and two deliveries had already depleted her physical resources. I didn't know if she would pull through.

"The second baby was also in trouble. She had been deprived of oxygen while the umbilical cord strangled her. The contractions drew the cord even tighter. Eventually, the doctor had to cut the cord while the baby was still inside Elise, then deliver the infant by coaxing its head through her birth canal with the doctor's hands.

Brian paused and breathed deeply.

"Elise will have a slow recovery," he said at last, "but she will make it through okay.

"The same is not true for Danielle, as we named our second child. The lack of oxygen flow to her brain resulted in Danielle suffering from a condition the doctors described as hypoxic-ischemic encephalopathy. As a result, Danielle will develop severe cerebral palsy. She will be a special needs child all her life."

The delivery room scene faded away to be replaced by a cozy family room setting. Elise, Brian and two approximately four-year-old girls were rolling a large rubber ball back and forth between them as they sat in a circle on the carpet. Elise stood up, and the rest of the scene froze around her.

ELISE: "We thank God every day for our two lovely children. They are both equally dear to us. Though each presents her own particular challenges, the joy they have brought into our lives is unimaginable.

"Despite medical odds to the contrary, God has answered our prayers for a child by providing us with not one, but two, beautiful babies.

"Praise be to God for the great gifts He has given us."

The scene, and the Courtroom, went dark.

CHAPTER 21
THE SIXTH DELIBERATION

After we had sat in darkness contemplating the two Testimonials for what seemed like an eternity, the Courtroom lighting returned to 'normal,' and the Judge was ready to address the Jury. Counsel stood behind their tables.

"Ladies and Gentlemen of the Jury.

Counsel for the Existence of God has advised the Court that she will be calling no further Witnesses during this trial. Therefore, you will shortly be departing for your final deliberation on new evidence.

"After this deliberation, Counsel will be presenting Final Arguments. Then you will have your last opportunity for discussion before determining your verdict.

"I advise you of these things now so that you can make the most of the deliberation time you have remaining. Soon you will be asked to reach your decision.

"The Court Officer will now escort you back to the Jury Assembly Room.

"Court is in recess."

The Judge pounded his gavel – the first time I had seen him use it. *Was he placing special emphasis on our responsibilities as the trial neared conclusion? Or was he sending some other message?*

This Judge had, thus far, been very deliberate about every detail of the trial. I couldn't help but think his use of the gavel at this stage had some intended consequence. I just couldn't figure out what it was.

As the Jury departed the Courtroom, the two Counsel and the Judge remained behind.

Back in the Assembly Room, Jurors searched for their seats in what had become a conditioned response. I located my table. Dariah and Ariel were already there. I bowed to Dariah and shook Ariel's hand.

Ariel's face had lost all semblance of the youthful exuberance it had held at the trial's outset. She was troubled and unsure.

Presently Tai arrived and our group was complete. He and I shook hands as he sat.

"From the Judge's final comments," I said, "I gather that we are to make the most of the time we have left in deliberations. So are we ready to dive in?"

I looked each of my table-mates in the eye. All were ready.

"Who would like to start?"

Tai was first to speak.

"If I recall correctly," he said, "this is the first time we have been asked to deliberate without the aid of any scientific evidence at all."

"Wasn't the psychologist a scientist?" Dariah asked.

"Not even close," Tai responded. "Psychology has never been considered a true science. It doesn't evaluate evidence using the scientific method. And its observations and conclusions are, for the most part, entirely subjective.

"I'm not nearly as comfortable evaluating this opinion testimony as I am dealing with scientific facts. What do you think about the psychologist's claim that we're all self-centered – at least to a degree – and that our self-centeredness should affect how we look at the evidence?"

I felt qualified to clarify.

"In the law, one must always consider the issue of 'burden of proof.' Whoever has that burden, has a more difficult job to win his case. If all evidence is equal, the party bearing the burden of proof will lose.

"Although you may not be aware of it," I said, to all three of my companions, "you are already familiar with at least one burden of proof circumstance. You know that, in the United States, a person is considered innocent until proven guilty.

"This means that the prosecutors have the burden of proving that the defendant is guilty. If they cannot convince a jury of the defendant's guilt, they have failed to meet their burden of proof, and the defendant goes free. The defendant doesn't have to prove anything. In theory, he can just sit there and still win the case.

"Does that clarify burden of proof?"

Everyone nodded understanding.

"So what the psychologist was saying, in legal terms, was that because humans are making the 'God' or 'No God' decision in this trial, and our self-centered nature inclines us to think of ourselves as the highest form of being, it is humans who should have the burden of proving that God *does not* exist, instead of requiring God to prove that He *does exist*.

"It's a concept that deserves some consideration."

"I now see what the psychologist was trying to say," Tai offered. "But I'm not sure that it will alter my verdict in any way."

"That is, of course, your decision," I said.

"Do either of you ladies want to discuss the psychologist's testimony further?"

They both shook their heads.

"But I am very interested in talking about the people who told their stories."

It was Ariel.

"It seems that they have suffered a lot. But they still believe in God. Why are they different from the first people we heard from – the African woman and the unfortunate young girl? That one poor man was a slave for ten years!

"Why aren't they mad at God?"

Dariah was first to respond.

"The last speakers we heard both said that they found comfort in

God. The first two did not. Is that not an important difference?"

I waited for someone else to speak. I didn't want to dominate the discussion.

Eventually Tai responded.

"Whether they felt comforted by God or not was all in their heads. The first two speakers were realistic. They recognized that their suffering meant that there could be no God. These last two were deluding themselves. They suffered through their pain until something good happened, then gave God the credit for the good stuff without blaming Him for all the pain along the way."

"Is that not the essence of faith?" Dariah asked.

"Call it faith. Call it mental defect. Call it what you want," Tai said. "The last two people – the slave and the childless mother – were living their lives on the Good Ship Lollipop. There was no reality in their perceptions.

"They suffered great anguish and never acknowledged that God was behind the pain. But when things got better, their happiness was all from God. Their perceptions were not at all realistic."

"I think Dariah's point about faith is a good one," I said. "Because of their faith that God was good, and that He was present in their lives, they perceived hope, not pain, in the tough times. And when things got better, they credited God with that as well. Their thinking is not delusional if one considers the constancy of their faith.

"But then we're back to the 'mystery of faith,' aren't we? Why do some have it and some not? I don't have any real insight into those questions."

"I'm glad I have been lucky to lead an easy life," Ariel said. "I don't know how I would survive what those people have gone through."

Tai couldn't resist a cruel comment.

"Well, it's time to wake up and smell the coffee, little girl. Everybody is going to have suffering. And after that, more suffering. You just haven't gotten there yet. My dad died when I was twenty. Just wait and your suffering will come, too. Then see how you feel about God."

Ariel looked terrified. I jumped in to defend her.

"Now, Tai. I'm sorry you lost your father so young. But that doesn't mean Ariel will lose hers. I don't see the need to try to frighten her into agreeing with you. The two of you are different people with different lives ahead of you. There's no need to belittle Ariel's beliefs because you are bitter."

Ariel appreciated my defense.

"Yeah, Tai," she said bravely. "Don't pick on me just because I'm a little younger than you and I'm maybe not so smart."

Tai chose not to argue further . . . which was just as well, because the Court Officer had returned to bring us back to the trial.

CHAPTER 22
CLOSING ARGUMENTS

When we returned to our pre-designated chairs in the Courtroom, I found that I had a front row seat for Counsel's Closing Arguments. I had been wondering what the summations would sound like.

Would the lawyers rehash the testimony so we remembered all the facts? Would they tie their closing remarks to their opening ones? Or would we be treated to something altogether different? Perhaps some new perspectives we may have not, as yet, considered?

I waited with anticipation as we went through the stand-up, sit-down, court-now-in-session routine.

JUDGE: "The attorneys will now present their closing arguments. As with the opening remarks, the attorneys' statements are not to be considered as evidence. If they introduce new facts which you have not heard from the Witnesses, you should disregard those statements of fact. Pay attention only to Counsel's recommendations regarding how you should view the evidence that has either been introduced by Witness testimony, or that was previously known to you from your own life experiences.

"Counsel for the Repudiation of God will speak first. Then Counsel for the Existence of God will follow. Please give each attorney your full attention. Their arguments may be helpful to you in deciding this case."

The Judge turned to Repudiation Counsel.

JUDGE: "Are you ready to begin, Counsel?"

COUNSEL FOR REPUDIATION: "Yes, Your Honor."

The general lighting faded to black as the bright circle followed the attorney from his Counsel Table to the lectern, which once again stood in the center of the open area before us.

Other than the dim presence of the Judge in the background, Counsel and the lectern were all that was visible. It shouldn't be too difficult to give him our attention when he was all we could sense or see.

He unbuttoned the collar of his white shirt and the front of his suit coat, then loosened his tie.

COUNSEL FOR THE REPUDIATION OF GOD'S CLOSING ARGUMENT

COUNSEL FOR REPUDIATION: "Ladies and Gentlemen of the Jury.

"Well. It has been a long day hasn't it?"

There were a few subdued acknowledgments from the Jury.

COUNSEL: "We've heard a number of academic experts – learned and respected persons all – who have presented a broad combination of facts and opinions for your consideration. We also saw that even the experts disagree on numerous issues within their respective areas of expertise.

"Did the universe begin as a result of natural forces? Was some supernatural Being at the start of it all? Or has the universe always existed?

"Does the fact that the earth possesses all necessary attributes to support human life mean that it was specifically designed just for us? Or is the habitability of earth simply a necessary condition for us to even ask the question – a rare natural coincidence which, had it not occurred, humans would not be here to marvel at its statistical improbabilities in the first place?

"Is the existence of God an imperative? Or a logical impossibility?

"One would think that, having debated this very question for at least centuries, and likely for millennia, humans would be coming gradually closer to a consensus opinion about God's existence, or his absence. But the opposite is true. Proponents of both sides of this issue have never possessed so much objective physical evidence to support their conclusions as they do today. Yet the disagreement is more polarized than ever.

"I, for one, grow weary of the argument. So I am hopeful that you will finally put this debate to rest.

"Let's start by looking at which facts our expert Witnesses agreed upon. Here are a few."

Counsel referred to a yellow notebook.

"Scientific experts have testified that:

- The universe began with a Big Bang Event which occurred approximately 13.7 billion years ago. Astronomers have actually observed galaxies that are more than 12 billion years old.
- The expansion and development of the universe, at least after the first fraction of a second, can be explained, by the laws of physics. For example, natural processes such as nuclear fusion occurring in the hearts of stars, formed all matter. Gravity organized the galaxies, stars and planets into the celestial array we see today.
- The earth is more than four billion years old. Archaeologists have positively dated earth rock specimens to an age of 3.9 billion years.
- The human species evolved at least several hundred million years ago. Numerous samples of human remains confirm this fact.
- Because of His purported abilities to transcend our universe, and to affect our consciousness, it is scientifically impossible to prove that any God might exist.

"Uncontroverted testimony by the professor of philosophy has established that it would be impossible for an all-knowing, all-loving, and all-powerful God to exist because:

- If God was all-powerful, this property would lead to

contradictions, as evidenced by the immovable rock and the irresistible force.

– If God was all-knowing, man could not have free will, because God would know every decision man made even before he made it. No one could ever make a different choice than the one God has foreseen.

– If God is all-loving and all-powerful, humans would not suffer as greatly as we have so vividly seen that they do.

"Furthermore, your own experience and common sense confirm the philosophy professor's arguments.

"Other Witnesses have agreed that:

– There are numerous discrepancies – errors, if you will – in Bible texts. There is no single, inspired, definitive document that can truly be called 'God's word.'

– Many wars have been fought, and countless lives extinguished, in the name of religion. God, if He exists, allows His name and apparent authority to be used in this way.

– If God exists, He permits extreme human suffering to occur. Theologians offer no logical explanation as to why this would be."

Counsel looked up from his notes.

"Besides the universal agreement among the experts to the facts I have just outlined, you will recall the request I made of each of you as this trial began. Look for evidence that God exists – for if He is among us, He will surely make His presence known.

"I don't know about you, but I watched very carefully, and I saw nothing even close to supernatural – no miracles, no speaking in tongues, no burning bushes, no changing water into wine, not even a lightning bolt or two.

"If there is a God, He doesn't care enough about you or me to make Himself known at the trial of His very existence. If He is a no-show here, how can He be present everywhere else?"

Counsel stepped around the side of the lectern and a pace or two closer to the Jury.

"With all of this agreement among the experts, and God himself being conspicuous in His absence from this trial, why does the argument that God exists still persist? What is there to argue about?

"For many, the answer is that the idea of God makes them feel safe and gives their lives a sense of purpose. The prospect of a life after earthly death gives them hope.

"These people have no proof to offer of God's existence, of course, because they will tell you that it cannot be proven. But they, nevertheless, cling to the 'God Fantasy' for the comfort it gives them.

"As the famous quote from Karl Marx states, 'Religion is the opiate of the masses.' People are addicted to their religion as irrationally as heroin addicts crave their poison. No amount of logic, reason or common sense can dissuade these religious addicts from their 'God Habit.'

"But rather than recognizing religion for the addiction that it is, the legions of believers legitimize their 'God Delusion' by giving it other names. 'Faith.' 'Belief.' 'A Divine Mystery.' 'Inspiration.' These are just a few of the ill-defined terms the religious masses use to mask their dependency.

"My friends. It is eminently clear that God is a delusion. Believers are fooling themselves. Ignorance is bliss – and this is especially true when a believer ignores God's absence.

"But delusion or not . . . why should the rest of us nonbelievers care?

"This is a fair question. But you already know the answers.

"Religious fanatics are dangerous. They assault family planning clinics. They terrorize the general populace with suicide bombings and threats of worse.

"Church institutions lobby unrelentingly for laws that would impose their religion upon all of us. One has only to look at legislation surrounding the legality of abortion, or of gay marriage, or of teaching creationism in the public schools, to see evidence of church interference.

"Furthermore, religion provides an excuse for the deranged mind to commit atrocities. As you have heard, many wars are fought in defense of God's causes.

"Far from being benign, the 'God Habit' can be lethal.

"In the interest of believers and nonbelievers everywhere, those who follow a God must learn the truth – even if it is not the delusional truth their addiction craves. That is why you are here. That is why you must act to protect all humans from the evils of religion. You must open the eyes of the world to this addiction.

"You must return a verdict that God *does not* exist.

"I have confidence in your abilities to do so."

Counsel stepped back behind the lectern and shuffled his notes to indicate that he was finishing.

"Thank you . . . each and every one of you . . . for your diligent service in this matter."

Counsel collected his materials from the lectern and returned to the Counsel Table. His light faded out.

The room remained dark for at least a minute after he had concluded his Argument. I assumed the dead time was intended to allow us to absorb what he had told us. But I was eager to hear the opposition Arguments, and filed the previous presentation in my mind for later consideration.

The light gradually brightened on Counsel for the Existence of God as she made her way to the podium.

COUNSEL FOR THE EXISTENCE OF GOD'S CLOSING ARGUMENT

Upon her arrival at the lectern, she paused for a few moments before speaking. Her head was bowed and her body still. *Praying? Or just centering herself for her presentation? I wasn't sure.*

Finally, she raised her face and looked at the Jury.

COUNSEL: "Does God exist?

"Why do we ask this question? And why has every generation in recorded history asked the same question?

"Does God exist?"

She paused a long moment.

"Is it because more than five billion religious residents of our planet suffer from a 'God Delusion,' as opposing Counsel would claim? And the unbelieving populace needs to cure us believers of our insidious 'God Addiction' before we do ourselves and the rest of the world irreparable harm?

"Is that why this issue keeps coming up . . . does God exist?

"Or is it because there remain certain characteristics of our existence that science cannot yet explain? How humans evolved from some ancient, nonliving, parent? How that evolution from inanimate beginnings happened in such a brief time? How humans became self-aware? Or what existed before our universe was born?

"Are these nagging questions the reason we ask: 'Does God exist?'

"Or is there something in the makeup of the human consciousness that causes us to search for our Creator? Has God, Himself, given us a genetic need to know Him? A built-in mechanism that requires us to search for God?

"Ladies and Gentlemen of the Jury.

"I confess that I do not know why we are compelled to ask if God exists. Nevertheless, that is the question of the ages. And it is the question you are asked to answer today.

"How should you go about finding your answer? What tools can you use to construct a solution to the God equation?

"Opposing Counsel suggests that, if God is here, He will make his presence obvious. There should be no doubt.

"I agree.

"I noted His presence here many times during this trial.

"His awesome power was evident in the cosmologists' descriptions of the scope and grandeur inherent in the cosmos. Billions of galaxies, each filled with billions of stars as potent, or more so, than our own sun.

"Nuclear furnaces consuming unimaginable amounts of

hydrogen and helium through atomic fusion. Dramatic supernovas exploding with such terrific force and immense energy that their brightness outshines the galaxies that contain them.

"These phenomena are clear evidence of God's almighty power. Scientists can labor to their heart's content, but no scientist can ever duplicate the power evident in the cosmos and its creation.

"While we are speaking of the cosmos, what better evidence of God's unlimited intelligence! Both cosmologists marveled at the complexities of the universe and its interwoven components.

"Furthermore, you heard the testimony of how delicately so many factors needed to be balanced in order for human life to exist. Our birth and survival in this almost entirely uninhabitable universe further testify to God's intelligence in designing a home for us in the vastness of the cosmos.

"And what of the marvel that is man? Is the birth of a child any less miraculous because science can understand *some* of the processes that cause an embryo to grow? And what scientist will claim to construct even simple life forms out of elemental dust? Much less possess the ability to make a human being from such components?

"Only God *can* make a tree – or a bird, or a fish or a human! No scientist can honestly explain the true origin of life – let alone replicate it.

"There was evidence, too, of God's compassion. We all saw the young man who was enslaved for more than ten years . . . beaten, whipped and forced to live with farm animals. Yet he praises God for his deliverance.

"And what of the young couple who were childless for many years, exhausting all human efforts to conceive? They felt God's comfort during their miscarriages, and gave thanks when, against all natural odds, they conceived twins. Though the mother nearly died in childbirth, and one of their daughters requires special care, yet they give thanks and praise to God for the gift of their children. This family offers clear testimony to His steadfast love and compassion.

"How could an unbiased observer not see God in these people's lives?

"God was certainly present at this trial. Of that, there can be no doubt. So opposing Counsel's demand is satisfied. You could render your verdict for God on that basis alone.

"But what other tools might you use to confirm God's existence?

"How about purpose?

"Without God, what is the purpose for the universe? Did the cosmos come into existence in a blaze of unimaginable power and glory, and live a vibrant existence without discernable goals for billions of years, only to expand infinitely – to die as a cloud of space dust?

"What a waste that would be. And what sense would it make?

"Without God, what is your individual purpose for living? To achieve safety and comfort? To hold the dogs of war at bay? To allow your children to survive, only for them to founder in the same purposeless void?

"If there is to be a purpose of any kind in all of this creation, there must be a God to provide that purpose and to allow for hope."

Counsel interlaced her fingers, resting her chin on her fists for a moment, as if in thought. Then she returned her hands to the edges of the lectern.

"But what of the tools of logic and reason? They are important to many of us – perhaps to all of us. Do they contradict God's existence? Do they somehow negate all that we know in our hearts and minds to be true?

"No.

"They merely fall short of comprehending God's complexity. And that limitation should not be surprising, given that God transcends the dimensions of our universe. If we could logically understand God, then humans would be as wise as God. Applying reason, logic and common sense to this proposition, we would have to conclude that humans could *never* fully understand God. But that fact does not argue for God's absence – only for his transcendent glory.

"Do we demand full comprehension of the sun before we venture out into its warmth and splendor? Or a require complete understanding of our cell phones before we make a call? Must we know why a song makes us happy? Or sad? Or a work of art calls forth emotion?

"Of course not.

"So why do we demand complete understanding of God? It is beyond all logic, reason and common sense to do so.

"Ladies and Gentlemen of the Jury.

"In deliberating over the issue of God's existence, you need to employ all of these tools. Consider God's power and intelligence as shown throughout the cosmos. Consider God's compassion as evidenced in the lives of the slave man and the young childless couple. Consider the issue of purpose on both a cosmic and personal scale. Use your own logic, reason and common sense to aid you. But don't expect your understanding of God through your limited mental faculties to be complete. You are not God. And your minds will never fully understand Him or His ways.

"Lastly, consider your own experiences with God, both inside and outside of this Courtroom. Consider your faith, in whatever stage it may be. Ask yourself whether your beliefs ring true. Explore your personal relationship with God and ask Him for guidance. See if He doesn't make your decision for you.

"I know that the evidence laid before you has, at times, been confusing. You have experienced conflicts between your heart and your mind. The verdict you must decide is weighty beyond comprehension. Yet this decision is your burden to bear.

"Like opposing Counsel, I have complete confidence that the members of this Jury are up to the task of rendering a considered verdict. You are nearing the conclusion of your part in this trial. Finish strong. Don't decide based on peer pressure, or upon your level of comfort, or the lack thereof.

"Look God in the eye and acknowledge His existence to all mankind.

"Thank you for your service."

The light on the woman attorney faded to black as she returned to her table.

As with the first closing, there were several moments of darkness in the Courtroom to allow us to consider the arguments she had made.

CHAPTER 23
THE SEVENTH DELIBERATION

When we returned to the Assembly Room, the seating arrangements had changed once more. This time, there were tables for six, instead of four. We all still needed to locate our assigned seats at the tables – which I did.

Considering the personnel with whom I had been deliberating thus far, it came as no surprise to me that my table included Tai, Clete, Dariah, Ariel and Kimi. At first this seemed appropriate. Then I began to wonder. *If the deliberation groups all consisted of six people, with whom had my absent companions deliberated when we met in groups of four?*

While I considered this puzzle, Ariel initiated the discussion – her voice verging on panic.

"You guys have got to help me figure this out. I'm so confused. When the man finished talking, I was positive that he was right – God hadn't shown up for the trial. But then when the woman spoke, I wasn't so sure."

"All my life I have believed in Jesus. But the things I have seen and heard today have got me all turned around. I want to get my vote right. You've *got* to help me understand!"

Her eyes welled with tears as she spoke.

"We're all in the same boat, Ariel," Tai said. "We've all seen the same evidence and heard the same arguments. To me, the decision is pretty straightforward. I didn't see God in there."

He pointed toward the Courtroom.

"And I didn't find God in here either. I mean no disrespect to those of you who will disagree."

He glanced at both Kimi and Dariah.

"I just haven't heard anything to change my opinion that God is not necessary or relevant in the world."

Dariah spoke.

"Tai. You are a man of hard facts. Does it not trouble you that so many billions of people believe in God's existence? And nonbelievers are only a small minority?"

Tai remained resolute.

"You have maybe heard the old saying that half the world is below average?" he said. "The fact that most people are unable to think and reason at a high level does not discount my ability to do so. I do not condemn those who are less intelligent than I. But at the same time, I certainly don't need to adopt their perceptions or beliefs."

"Well now, Tai," Clete said.

I could almost see the hair bristling on Clete's neck.

"Just how many of us at this table do you figure are dumber than you?"

"I'm not trying to make this personal, Clete. I'm speaking in terms of the masses."

"Of which there are six at this table," Clete replied. "If you're not gonna show your pompous attitude for what it is, somebody's got to. I think you're fulla yourself and you don't give a flyin' fur ball about anybody else or what they might believe."

Tai started to stand up to confront Clete. Ariel cowered in her chair between the two men. I needed to intervene.

"Tai. Sit down! We're not going to have any fist fights.

"And Clete, I know it's been a long day, but let's try to keep it civil through this last deliberation."

I gave each of them a steely stare. Tai sat down. Clete made a grunting sound and crossed his arms over his chest. I took these signs as a minor victory for reason.

"Now . . . we've heard Tai's opinion," I said. "And we know Ariel would like some help with her decision. Does anyone have any thoughts that might be helpful to Ariel, and for that matter, to the rest of us?"

Dariah spoke again.

"All during the trial, I have been praying to Allah for faith and wisdom. My heart tells me that Allah is with me. But my mind fights my heart. I have never before considered these things . . . these arguments I have heard . . . these stories that have been revealed today. I confess that I do not yet possess the wisdom to have comfort in my understanding of this trial.

"Ariel. You are not alone in your struggles.

"But is faith not something more than the things our eyes can see? Than the thoughts our minds can perceive?

"I still have faith. But I question the strength of my conviction. I wonder . . . only a small bit . . . whether I hold to my faith for the sake of my own comfort. Allah, forgive my doubts. But my mind betrays my heart and argues with it over my faith.

"I must pray more fervently before I am able to answer the question of this Court."

Ariel did not appear comforted by anything she had heard thus far. I thought of my own daughters, Annie and Shannon, and believed I understood Ariel's sense of being overwhelmed by this decision.

"Ariel," I said, "I liked the tools the woman attorney urged us to use to evaluate whether God exists. Each of us will find some of those tools more helpful, and some less so. I believe this is because we are all different people from diverse backgrounds. And we carry with us the wisdom gained from our own, unique experiences.

"I have only known you for a few hours, Ariel. But if I may make a suggestion, I would recommend that you concern yourself less with what you *understand* to be true, and more with what you *feel* to be true. If I were you, I would follow what my heart tells me is right, and not be confused or panicked by evidence your mind does not have the ability to comprehend.

"To be clear, I do not say that you should ignore any of the evidence. I only believe it will be easier for you to reach into yourself for the answer, rather than for you to let your common sense give way to arguments you don't understand . . . that none of us truly understands.

"Do you find that at all helpful?"

"Thank you," Ariel said, still teary, but somewhat less upset. "I'm not really sure I understand exactly what you're saying. But it makes sense to me on some level, I guess."

"I've still got my strategy in place," Clete announced. "I wasn't sure about it for a while. But now I'm confident. I'm votin' for God, 'cause I got nothin' to lose. It's a sure bet.

"I gotta admit, this has been one interesting experience. Don't believe I ever learned so much in one day in my whole life. Mainly about people and the world, though. Not so much about God."

Kimi had been conspicuous in her silence.

"So, Kimi," I asked, "do you have anything you'd like to put on the table for discussion?"

"Thank you for your consideration, Mr. William. But I do not believe I have any thoughts that will be useful to the rest of you. My beliefs, my experiences, are so different from yours. I am not sure how to say what I feel."

"C'mon little lady," Clete prodded. "Don't be shy. Let's hear what you're thinkin'."

Kimi looked at each of us, her face tilted slightly downward.

"I will say what I am able, Mr. Clete. But please do not be disappointed if it makes no sense to you."

Kimi placed her folded hands on the table in front of her and raised her chin just a bit.

"In the tradition of my people, there has never been a question such as we are asked today. The Great Spirit has always been known to us. We have no reasons to doubt.

"He is in the sparkling of the waters. He is in the forest mist. His footprints are the footprints of my people. When all is silent around us, we hear Him speak – in the whisper of the wind, or the squirrel's chatter.

"I know you cannot believe me when I say such things. But I see the Great Spirit in all living creatures. In all of you at this table. He is in your eyes, in your words, in your actions.

"So when I am asked, 'Does God exist?' it is a question that is strange to me. But perhaps that is because I am not as intelligent as Mr. Tai, or as bold and confident as Mr. Clete. Or it may be because I am not as devout as Ms. Dariah, or as filled with hope and wonder as Miss Ariel. Or as wise as Mr. William.

"Perhaps I am ignorant. But for me, I *know* that God exists. And I can think of no argument, and no evidence, that could change that which I know to be true.

"I apologize if my words are not useful to this discussion."

Kimi possessed qualities of confidence, innocence and wonder that I deeply respected. I found myself wishing I could see with Kimi's eyes.

"That was beautiful, Miss Kimi," Clete said, in a tone more humble than I had heard in his voice before.

At this point, the Court Officer appeared in the Assembly Room doorway. It was time to cast our votes.

CHAPTER 24
THE VERDICT

In a typical trial, before any voting occurred, all the Jurors would sit around a large table and hash out their disagreements until a unanimous verdict could be reached. However, given the unusual nature of the trial thus far, I was not surprised when the Court Officer told us that we would be voting individually, without further discussion or consultation among ourselves.

The Officer explained that one of the four corner alcoves had been converted into a sort of 'voting booth.' The Officer would call our names from his list. Then each of us, in turn, would enter the voting booth and declare our verdict by following the directions we found therein. When we finished voting, we would return to the Courtroom and await completion of the balloting process.

When the Officer finished speaking, the room was silent. No chairs creaked. There was no coughing, talking or clearing of throats. All sat perfectly still awaiting the vote.

The Court Officer perused his list of Jurors, then raised his eyes, his gaze resting on someone in the back left corner of the room. Although I hadn't heard a name called, a man rose from his seat and proceeded solemnly to the alcove. The rest of us remained quiet. I'm not sure I could have spoken or moved if I had wanted to.

My thoughts focused on the vote I was about to cast. It was not an easy decision for me. I had been raised in the Lutheran Church. I knew all the Bible stories.

But I was also an intelligent person. And an attorney – part of a legal system whose ultimate goal is finding "Truth." How should I balance the ill-defined belief I had in a Christian God with the scientific realities that seemed to render God unnecessary – or even unlikely?

As I continued contemplating my vote, the first man exited the alcove and started toward the Courtroom door. Another Juror . . . this time a woman . . . rose and headed toward the voting booth. I hadn't heard her name called either.

Was this another of the Judge's histrionics? Did each of us have a small speaker in our chair so we could hear our name when called? Or perhaps the Officer was using a highly focused parabolic speaker – one that projected sound in only a very specific direction?

I was glad that I was not one of the first to vote. I was still conflicted.

Occasionally, I thought, *I pray to God for the safety of my family or friends. Why would I do that if I didn't believe God exists? Yet I certainly didn't believe in God enough to trust that he would provide for my wife and me in our retirement. I had been saving steadily so I could provide for myself.*

And what about all the suffering in the world? How could that be part of God's plan?

We had been discussing these very subjects all day long and the problems seemed insoluble. How could anyone prove God exists or doesn't exist? In the end, it all depended on faith – didn't it? And what is faith, after all, but a belief in the unknowable?

At that moment, I actually prayed for faith. But I didn't really expect to receive it. *How foolish,* I thought, *to pray to a God that you don't expect to answer your prayer. And how much more foolish would it be to actually expect an answer?*

The woman had left the booth for the Courtroom. Several others followed her in succession. Their names never heard. Their votes cast. Their solemn walks to the Courtroom.

How different, I thought, from the atmosphere during our first deliberation as a Jury. There had been laughter, anger, disbelief, astonishment, a sense of the absurd. And nothing had really changed since then – at least as far as our mission was concerned. We were trying the existence of God. Still a bizarre notion, a ridiculous task for a court of law. And the proceedings since that first deliberation had done nothing to make any sane person think this endeavor any less foolish . . . or any more real.

Yet here we sat, seriously contemplating voting for, or against, God. I wondered how I had come to consider this vote a monumental task, rather than a ridiculous whim. And I wondered how everyone else had been lured to the same deliberate conclusion.

I heard my name called and rose from the table. My head was still spinning. And I hadn't yet decided how my vote should be cast.

I moved to the corner booth.

When I entered the alcove, I saw before me a human-size, bronze statue of Lady Justice. With her eyes blindfolded, she held a sword at her right side and the scale of justice in her left hand. On the lamp stand that had always been in the alcove, there were two, small, circular wooden boxes, each containing a supply of either white or red marbles. On the box with the white marbles was written "GOD." On the other box, "NO GOD."

I'm not sure how I knew what to do, but with no small amount of trepidation, I selected my marble and placed it on one side of the scale of liberty. I saw no other marbles on either side of the scale. That seemed odd.

As soon as I had deposited my marble, a woman appeared in the alcove entrance. She was fair-skinned with blond hair and wore a floor-length, formal red gown. She reached out her arm, beckoning me to follow. I extended my hand to accept hers. She led me across the Assembly Room and to the Courtroom hallway.

Without a word, she pointed toward the Courtroom. I took a few steps in that direction and then looked back. The woman was gone. *Why had I received an escort from the voting booth when no one else had?*

The Courtroom was now lit by luminescence from a ceiling that represented earth's view of the universe – probably as depicted by the Hubble Space Telescope. No planetarium could have projected a more clear or more layered stellar array.

Purplish nebulae swirled among spiral galaxies. A few planets appeared impossibly close. The repeating strata of stars and galaxies receded infinitely into the distance.

Although there were no other light sources, the illumination from the ceiling was sufficient for me to find my seat next to the man who had voted before me. I sat, but still felt no desire to speak.

When at last all Jurors had returned to the Courtroom, a shaft of light from somewhere above us shone down on the doorway to the Judge's Chambers. The Judge was already sitting in his wheelchair as the light hit him. He slowly wheeled himself past the ramp to his Bench and continued toward the center of the Courtroom – where the lectern had once stood.

It seemed to me that his passage across the Courtroom floor was labored. His face was gaunt and tired. He no longer projected the air of authority that had pervaded his presence on the Bench. As he wheeled himself ever closer, I saw that his chair now had foot rests, and on them, bronze-armored boots extended from beneath the black robe.

The Judge came to a stop not ten feet from the front row of Jurors. The shaft of light from its unknown source in the heavens had followed him there. His breathing was labored beneath the robe, and his bony-thin hands clutched the rigid arms of the wheelchair.

After a long moment, he reached back to lock the chair's spoked wheels. Then, with trembling arms, he raised himself to a standing position before us, steadying himself on a wooden cane that had been hidden in the folds of his robe.

He spoke in a voice that resonated more with comfort than with the weakness I had expected, given his depleted appearance.

"Ladies and Gentlemen of the Jury.

"We have come to the end of the trial. This is my last opportunity to speak with you. As I told you from the outset, this has been no ordinary trial. And the verdict is no ordinary verdict.

"I am certain that many among you will be disappointed to hear that the sum of your votes will not be disclosed to you. That is, your collective vote will remain a secret from your minds."

There was some whispering and mumbling from Jurors at this announcement.

"But do not despair. Your service has been of value. You have deliberated questions that challenge your most fundamental beliefs. In God. In nature. In science. In man. You have considered these things and have reached your decisions – right or wrong.

"And make no mistake, in this trial there is, and always has been, a right verdict and a wrong one, as you must have surmised at one point or another.

"Either God exists, or He does not."

The Judge's statement was so matter-of-fact that it caught me off-guard. Trials are for the purpose of finding the truth when it is not yet known. It had actually not occurred to me that we were contemplating a circumstance with an objective outcome.

So much of the legal system is judgment, opinion, weighing of one piece of evidence against another. The thought had not crossed my mind that this trial was different in that respect . . . though I confess that it should have been obvious from the outset that we, the Jurors, had no authority to alter the reality of God or the cosmos with our verdict.

Why hadn't I thought of that earlier?

We were never trying God's existence. It was our individual beliefs that were on trial. That was why no collective verdict would make sense. We had chosen a verdict for ourselves only.

I felt stupid for not seeing the end-game sooner. Our deliberations had been tools for self-examination – not attempts to find consensus.

Or were they also something more?

The Courtroom lighting blinked out. Darkness and silence

surrounded me.

CHAPTER 25
MY CONVERSATION WITH THE JUDGE

When the darkness lifted, I found myself alone with the Judge in a circle of light, maybe eight feet in diameter. My Juror's seat had become an upholstered, high-backed chair. A black, wooden coffee table separated me from the Judge in his wheelchair.

Styrofoam cups of coffee stood on the table in front of each of us. The Judge's bronze 'legs' were gone and his wheelchair was, again, without footrests.

"Mr. Kensey. I am here to tell you," the Judge continued, "that God does exist. He exists. He is almighty. And He loves mankind more than any creature in the universe.

Man is, indeed, made in God's image. And God's aspirations for man are great. But so are His frustrations with human stubbornness, arrogance and disbelief."

I was looking around for evidence that the other Jurors were there somewhere. I could neither see nor hear them.

"It is just you and I now, Mr. Kensey. The trial is over. The rest of the Jury has departed. You no longer need to maintain your Courtroom demeanor. We are just two sentient souls having a conversation."

"May I ask a question, Your Honor?"

"Certainly. Ask what you will."

The Judge leaned forward and picked up his coffee cup, taking a sip and then resting it in a holder near one arm of his chair.

I had many questions, but none more worrisome than this first one.

"Your Honor, where did the other Jurors go?"

"Mr. Kensey. Up to this point, the other Jurors have had very much the same experience of this trial as you have had – though they have struggled with their own challenges, some similar to yours, and some very different.

"But that is not the question you have asked. You worry about what has happened to the people you got to know here today. That is commendable to be sure. And though this information is not truly relevant to your mission, I will share the details of their departures with you.

"Of the thirty-six, one-third have been called to heaven to be with the Almighty, to live forever in the peace and splendor of His presence. The remainder have returned to their daily lives with no specific recollection of today's trial – but with a vague need to find answers to the questions of suffering, science and faith by which they are regularly troubled."

"And the twelve who were called . . . what has become of their lives, their families, their friends?"

"The perception of all surrounding these twelve is that they have died suddenly, tragically, with no logic to explain their deaths. But the Almighty will comfort the survivors if they seek His comfort. And the lives of all who knew these twelve will have been enriched by the experience."

"So they're dead?"

I knew it sounded accusatory. But the unfairness of it all was overwhelming, and I had reacted before thinking.

"That is the impression those of the world will have, yes. But the truth is that the chosen third have ascended beyond death's reach.

"Is this difficult for you to understand, Mr. Kensey? One who should know that the soul of the believer transcends death and lives eternally with the Father in heaven?"

The Judge again sipped his coffee, as though this life and death discussion were a friendly chat – and one that he had had before.

I knew the 'right' answer. This question should not be unsettling to me. That some of my fellow Jurors had died and gone to heaven should not be a challenge for me to comprehend. I had learned that 'truth' long ago – first from my parents, and then again in confirmation classes.

But this situation no longer resembled doctrinal recitation. It was very possible that someone I had met today was dead – taken from his or her parents, children, friends – as a result of this proceeding.

I felt sick. I had participated in a minor holocaust.

"I perceive your struggles, Mr. Kensey. But your perspective is flawed. Departing this world for an eternal existence with the Divine is man's ultimate achievement. It is not to be mourned, but celebrated.

"As I have said, those who seek comfort for their loss of a friend or family member will receive it – in full measure. Why do you still torment yourself at their ascendance?"

Again, I knew the 'right' answer. Instead I lashed out.

"Because they're dead! That's what torments me."

The Judge looked at me across the coffee table with a measure of pity.

"You need time to think on these things. Then if you seek God's comfort, you, too, shall receive it. It is asking much for you to fully comprehend right now. Your life has not been lived around such beliefs."

I was infuriated that the Judge would treat me like a child . . . telling me that I could not comprehend.

"Mr. Kensey, the fate of today's Jurors is the same as the fate of each Jury that has served in every trial before today's. And such will be the result in many trials yet to come."

"So this trial has not been the only one of its kind?"

"I have presided over many millions of such trials over the past thousands of years. To judge is my honor and sacred obligation."

Was Judgment Day not one single day at all? Was it instead a series of Judgment Days on an ever-rolling calendar? The thought was beyond my ken.

"I know that you are still troubled. But we must move forward in our discussion. We can dwell on this issue of death no longer. Be at peace, so that you may fulfill your purpose and know your path."

My anger with the Judge faded from my mind. New questions filled my consciousness.

"Why am I the only one of the thirty-six who remains here with you? I voted for God's existence, as I'm sure did many others. Why have I not departed to return to my life?"

"Mr. Kensey. You, among all the Jurors, are particularly suited to an important mission that must be carried out. God has called you to this mission. And you will voluntarily serve once I have explained it to you.

"Are you willing to hear of your special calling?"

I really wished this whole nightmare was over. But I saw no exits. So I decided to hear the Judge out – learn God's 'mission' for me.

"I will listen," I said. "And then I will decide whether to participate."

"Thank you, Mr. Kensey. I will now explain your purpose and why God has interrupted your life for this mission."

CHAPTER 26
THE MISSION

"From the beginning, when the Almighty first gave man a soul, man has been stubborn and disobedient. Man has never been satisfied being man. He lusts to be God – an aspiration he can never achieve. So for the most part, man has chosen to separate himself from God . . . to make his own way in the world.

"Because man is a creature of limited intelligence and limited abilities, he has, understandably, failed miserably in his attempts to rule the world without God. His many failings have led to grievous human suffering and poor stewardship of the earth, and have allowed all manner of evil to pervade creation.

"There is no room for God in the world of man's making. Man has set up barriers to even recognizing God's glory – to having faith and trust in God's supreme power and love. These barriers – these impediments to finding God – are not easy for man, himself, to conquer.

"This is partly true because man has made the barriers invisible. They escape the discernment of his mind. He is like the sick person who does not perceive his illness, and therefore, refuses to seek medical attention. He dies while his cure lies within his own reach.

"To be specific, man has set up five invisible obstacles to establishing a personal relationship with God. Though most men will not recognize these obstacles in themselves, it will be your mission to help men see their own roadblocks, and thus regain for themselves a rightful relationship with their Father, the Creator."

I remained skeptical, though given all I had witnessed today, one might wonder why.

"Suppose I agree to hear more, and to undertake this 'mission,' as you call it, how can I make men see the invisible or perceive the indiscernible? Why am I so specially suited for this task?"

"During this trial, you have observed and identified these human failings that are the greatest obstacles to faith. You already know them. And because of your gift for argument and explanation – the same gift that has made you a successful lawyer – you are able to convey your understanding to humanity."

The Judge paused.

"I perceive that you do not yet comprehend fully the obstacles of which I am speaking. And you do not trust me to impart them to you accurately. Nevertheless, please allow me to continue, that you might know and understand."

I had come this far. And I was intrigued by the Judge's statement that I had already identified the obstacles. I would listen a while longer.

"Please. Enlighten me."

I could hear a tone of hubris in my voice as I spoke these words. I didn't like hearing it. But my words had been spoken and I could scarcely take them back at this point.

"Thank you, again, Mr. Kensey, for your patience with me. Please listen carefully, for these are the five obstacles to attaining faith, and how you will recognize each.

"The first obstacle is Anger.

"You have Witnessed Anger in the young atheist metal worker who said he would never believe in God because he saw hypocrisy in the church. He had encountered people in his life who attended church regularly. But despite their pious words, they had not lived their lives according to God's will. Rather they had wielded the Bible as a weapon, bringing it to bear against all those they perceived as sinners.

"Even this young man's parents had shown their hypocrisy by forcing him to attend church throughout his youth, and then abandoning the church once he had left their home.

"You saw his Anger and the reasons he could not have faith. But he could not see this obstacle. Even when he was shown that all religions believe in the same things he does – and that all people are imperfect and betray their beliefs, including himself – he would still not consider welcoming God into his life. His Anger at the hypocrisy of the church and its members was too great and too well-ingrained."

"I did recognize the things you have said about this man," I responded. "But what could I say to help him see his own Anger?"

"For most men, to gently counsel regarding their obstacles will allow them to perceive their shortcomings. They may not acknowledge that perception. But they will know it in their hearts. Whether they act on that knowledge is up to them. They have the free will to hold onto their Anger, or to release it and allow faith to take root."

"But how will I be able to 'gently counsel' men such as the young metal worker? I don't even know the man. And if I were to chance upon him, he wouldn't want to speak to a stranger."

"That is why you will write of this trial, Mr. Kensey. Your account will be your Witness. All who read your words will have their eyes opened to their challenge. They will hear why they have such a challenge. And they will choose whether to seek God despite their barriers."

"So I am to write about the trial?"

"Yes. But please allow me to continue. You need to learn all five obstacles before we can move on."

I allowed the Judge to proceed with his lecture, and myself to take a sip of the coffee.

"The second obstacle is Fear.

"Society scorns people of faith. It has always been so. Jesus was the ultimate example. He suffered humanity's disdain and mockery even to his death. Many others suffer this affliction of society, even today, when they speak of God.

"When a scientist steps forward and admits her faith, she faces ridicule among her colleagues. They call her 'weak-minded,' 'illogical' and 'unscientific' – all words that cut deeply into the identity of a person of her profession.

"You will write of the brave scientists who have advocated for God at this trial, and of the others who would rather attribute creation to a 'fairy' than admit the possibility of a Supreme Being.

"In these accounts, scientists and members of other professions who value their intellectual reputations, will recognize Fear as their obstacle to faith. They will either surmount it, or not . . . as they have free will. But the knowledge of their impediment will give them a fresh chance to choose faith.

"The third obstacle," the Judge continued, "is Ego.

"You heard from the psychologist today that all men are selfish. Many already recognize their own selfishness and have, nevertheless, chosen to reject faith despite that knowledge. Many more have recognized their selfish nature and overcome the need to place themselves first in all that they do and all that they believe.

"In your account of this trial, readers will see selfishness in Clete, who will cast his vote for the verdict that guarantees that he will prevail. And they will see selfishness in Counsel's admonition to demand that God provide evidence to prove His own existence.

"Who is man to demand anything more of God? Your readers will be forced to view man's egoistic nature for what it is. Then they will decide for themselves who should bear the burden of proving God's existence.

"The fourth obstacle is Idolatry.

"Since the days before Moses, men have worshiped idols. They have kept icons in their homes, or over their doors. They have used crystals to ward off evil spirits. Today's idols are more insidious than such ancient symbols.

"Although men have always pursued wealth and possessions, modern society places a higher value than ever before on conspicuous displays of luxury and obvious commercial consumption. You, yourself, have several idols."

I had been listening intently and was taken aback by this statement.

"And which idols might those be?" *Damn! I had sounded cocky again.*

"You value your intelligence and your ability to reason – both gifts from the Almighty – far more than your faith in God.

"Consider your own struggles with logic regarding the philosopher's testimony. Note how eloquently you undermined the cosmologist's statistics. Even at the moment you cast your vote, a final appeal to reason would have sufficed to change your verdict.

"If you doubt me, consider this. Would you sooner give up your ability to think and reason at a very high level, or your faith in God?"

He stopped and watched me for the shortest of moments. I failed to respond.

"You see?" he said. "Even now . . . having seen and heard all of which I speak . . . you still hesitate to choose your God.

"But you have another idol as well . . . money. You have saved quite a lot of it. "And I daresay that, even now, you do not trust God to provide for you, preferring instead to place your faith in your investment advisor."

"I don't think that's really a fair statement," I said. "I give generously to the church. Doesn't God want my family to have financial security?"

"With God, you need no further security.

"But as I have said, one can only expose the impediment. Ultimately the choice is yours to make."

I knew I had spoken defensively. But to give up our family savings and financial security . . . . It was a lot to ask.

"I must point out," the Judge continued, "that the amount of your wealth has nothing to do with your Idolatry. Kimi is far wealthier than you – even by earthly measures. But she would willingly part with her possessions to serve her God. That is the difference. Money is not an idol for those who place their trust in God."

He paused to let this last statement sink in.

"Are we ready to proceed?"

"Yes," I said.

"The fifth obstacle is Comfort."

"Comfort?" I'm sure I sounded incredulous.

"Yes. You can see why this impediment to faith can be particularly insidious."

"I can understand why no one would recognize Comfort as an impediment to faith. But Comfort . . . insidious? I don't see it."

"Many are comfortable with their faith in God – or their lack of it. When one is comfortable with the *status quo*, one has no incentive to pursue change.

"You of all people, Mr. Kensey, must realize that attending church doesn't make you a Christian any more than standing in a garage makes you a car. Faith must be alive. Like any belief, faith requires constant challenges to remain relevant. It is the challenge that makes the belief vital, and therefore, stronger.

"Among your friends on the Jury, Ariel is an example of someone who is comfortable in her faith. She 'knows about Jesus.' But she doesn't know enough – or question her faith enough – to be able to withstand logical arguments against God. Nor would she be able to recognize false teachings were she to encounter them.

"And Tai is an example of a man who is comfortable in his atheism. He has no need of God. He would not recognize a miracle if he called it forth himself. He has closed his mind to further consideration of God – mainly because it would cause him discomfort.

"The theologian who testified about all the mistakes in the New Testament . . . he is a sad example. He became so comfortable with his faith in the literal translation of the Bible, that he lost faith entirely when he discovered that scriptural wording has changed through different times and for diverse cultures. Though he researched the Bible extensively, and no doubt could provide numerous Biblical citations to defend his childhood Christianity, his adult endeavors were directed solely at bolstering his 'comfortable' faith in his own abilities – not at drawing himself closer to his Creator.

"Had he been willing to question his rigid belief in literalness, perhaps he could have been open to an understanding of scriptures that allows for Biblical wording to change – or even to appear inconsistent from one passage to another.

"Both Ariel and this theologian suffer the same affliction of being comfortable in their immature faith. Perhaps if, while Ariel is still young, someone shows her why she needs to question her faith, and understand it beyond rote recitation, she will take on the challenge of discomfort, and thus draw nearer to God.

"Of course, as I have repeatedly stated, whether to embrace challenges will be her decision once she understands that her Comfort is an obstacle to the full development of her faith."

I considered the Judge's statements. If these five attributes, or conditions, or states of being, or whatever you wanted to call them, were indeed obstacles to faith, I wondered if I, myself, would be able to overcome them. Or if my words would suffice to identify them to others.

"Do not be concerned about your own abilities," the Judge said, answering my doubt before I had even raised it. "With the Almighty, all things are possible. God will help you through your challenges to tell this story. Whether you will then have faith . . . Mr. Kensey . . . is a matter of your own free will."

My doubts about my competence for the 'mission' remained. But I also had another nagging question.

"You are wondering about the problem of 'suffering.' Theologians, philosophers, and discerning students of faith have all asked this question. 'If God loves us, and He is all-powerful, why is there suffering in the world?'

"For God to give a complete answer to this question, humans would need a greater capacity to understand the ways of God. But here are several facts you might want to think about.

"First of all, consider God's own suffering when his children – and all people are his children – choose to denounce Him and to harm one another. The Almighty has given His chosen ones only two commands: 'Show respect and deference to your Creator'; and 'Love your fellow man as you do yourself.'

"In return for these two simple requests, God provides his unwavering love. His love for mankind is greater than that of a mother for her children. When the child suffers, how much more does the mother feel the child's pain?

God most certainly *does not cause human suffering*. Yet God allows suffering as a necessary part of free will – even though He suffers most of all.

"Also consider the opposite of suffering – Comfort. Have we not already addressed the insidious nature of Comfort? If mankind experiences nothing but Comfort through all of his days, will he ever know – or even have reason to seek out – his God?

"I know that these answers do not satisfy your mind. But believe this . . . God does not want His children to suffer. And in times of pain and anguish, His true comfort is always there for the asking."

"I still don't understand why there has to be *so much* suffering," I said. "But according to you, I am not able to comprehend a complete answer to that question."

"That is correct, Mr. Kensey. For it is written, 'The ways of God are foolishness unto men.' So it has always been. So it will always be."

I considered all that the Judge had told me. My mission seemed an insurmountable undertaking. Yet under the circumstances, I felt I should not – perhaps, could not? – decline the task.

"Okay. If I accept this mission of yours, what do I need to do?"

"Live your life and search for God's purpose at every opportunity."

"I'm still not sure I have the faith to pull off what you are asking me to do. Even though I *believe* God will help me, I can't seem to *trust* that He will.

"Do you suppose I could see just one miracle to give my faith a boost?"

It had sounded just as stupid when I said it as when I had first decided to ask.

The Judge laughed.

"You have seen more miracles today than most men see in a lifetime. Yet you require another. You can understand why the Father's patience is sometimes challenged.

"But I will humor you once again. I know that you are a difficult man to convince. So I will show you a miracle that you cannot deny.

"I will show you the beginning."

"The beginning of what?"

"The beginning of the universe. The birth of the cosmos."

Before I could say anything further, the ceiling was, once more, illuminated with stars and galaxies and colorful stellar dust. As I watched, all of the sky that was stretched out before me began to shrink – receding into itself. As it shrank, my viewpoint moved with it, approaching ever nearer to the center of the collapsing cosmos.

As the stars around me bunched closer and closer together, I could feel a pull – a sort of suction – tugging me toward the barely visible vortex at the center of everything.

The pull became stronger and stronger. Galaxies swirled and disappeared as if down a celestial drain. Soon I was among them – swirling, stretching, shrinking until . . . there was nothing.

The Courtroom, the Judge, the table and chairs, the starlit ceiling, even my body, were all gone. My consciousness floated aimlessly in a void – a nothingness.

Then there appeared a tiny glint of light in the darkness. It expanded rapidly toward me, around me. I saw the instant of creation played out in ultra-slow motion before my eyes – the first micro-milliseconds at the birth of all that is.

And I understood the nothingness that was everywhere, and the everything that was nowhere. I understood it all . . . and was in awe.

CHAPTER 27
AFTER THE TRIAL

I'm not sure how long I hung in space, mesmerized, watching creation unfolding before me. But when I was ready, I closed my eyes.

When I opened them again, I was driving my Lincoln sedan down Washington Avenue toward home. What a story I would tell to Jen when I arrived. And then I would start to write the book – accomplish my mission.

As I crossed Fourth Street, a horn blared and tires screeched to my left. I turned my head just in time to see the headlights of the armored car and feel my head smash against its chrome grill.

Then all was black.

* * *

Two months later.

"How is he doing this evening?" Jen's voice asked from the corridor outside my hospital room.

"Pretty much the same," a nurse answered.

"Do the doctors hold out any hope at all that he'll regain some semblance of normal brain function?"

"There's always hope, Mrs. Kensey. But I'm afraid no one is predicting a miracle anytime soon."

My wife pushed the door slowly open, taking care not to disturb me in case I was sleeping.

"Hi, Bill," she said in a voice far too cheerful for the circumstances. "How's it going today?"

She didn't wait for an answer. She knew I wasn't going to say anything.

She sat down beside my bed, where I lay propped up, my notebooks and clipboard on my lap, a ball point pen in my hand. I rotated my shoulders to face her and tried to smile. I couldn't feel my face move at all. I had grown accustomed to the lack of sensation.

"Still writing, I see. Are we about ready for publication?"

I handed her my completed manuscript – the culmination of my life's work. The story of the trial and of my encounter with God.

She reviewed it with exaggerated enthusiasm.

"Very nice. Very well written indeed."

Then she handed the notebooks back to me. Tears welled in her eyes.

"Sorry, Dear. I need to step into the hall for a minute."

She dabbed at her eyes with a tissue as she fled just outside the door.

"Is that all he does?" she asked the nurse. "Write in those notebooks?"

"Pretty much. Just 'God is good' over and over. He must have filled half-a-dozen notebooks by now."

* * *

As I was staring at the hospital room walls, saying my evening prayers, I felt his presence beside me again. The Judge had visited me every day since the accident. He was no longer confined to a wheelchair, nor showed signs of illness or affliction. In fact, his appearance was youthful – vibrant. I could never remember his facial features after he left my room. But I always recognized him when he appeared.

Tonight, he sat in a bedside chair and paged through my stack of notebooks, paying particular attention to the parts I had written just today.

"I see you've finished the manuscript, Mr. Kensey. Well done. I will see to its publication and distribution right away. You have done a great service for your Heavenly Father."

I felt a great sense of relief. My mission was complete. My writings had passed inspection.

"Do you have any remarks you would like to add for the end of the book?"

He knew I did.

I wrote the Epilogue as the Judge waited patiently.

When I was finished, the Judge took the extra pages from my lap. *Could I see it one last time,* I thought. *All of it.*

Judge Cole understood what I wanted, and returned the manuscript to me – all seven notebooks. I perused them as the Judge waited some more.

The book had turned out just as I had hoped it would. The Witnesses' testimony. The Jurors who'd shared my deliberations. The arguments of Counsel. Even my final chat with Judge Cole after the trial was over. All was as I had remembered it.

I said a silent prayer thanking God for his goodness and for His help in writing the book. I returned the notebooks to Judge Cole and tried again to smile.

He smiled at me, accepting the manuscript from my outstretched hands. Then he reached one strong hand toward me and gently laid it on my forehead.

"Sleep well, my son," he said, as I closed my eyes. "Your sins are forgiven."

EPILOGUE

Now that I have completed the book, I know that my writing weaknesses were never really important to this story. It was foolish of me to concern myself with my own shortcomings. My writings could never fail to deliver God's message because His inspiration transcends them.

For me, authoring this book has truly been a transcendental experience.

I have come to realize that we all believe in something. We all have faith in something. For some, it is in the wisdom of our own minds. But for me . . . my faith is in the One who created us in His image and who gave us the free will to choose.

God Almighty has shown me my obstacles. He has reached out His hand and comforted me through my challenges. I no longer covet wealth. I have come to understand the limitations of intellect and reason. And I am at peace.

I pray regularly that my family – Jen, Annie and Shannon – will come to the same enlightenment as I. I also pray that they will know that I do not suffer from my physical and mental disabilities. And that God *did not* cause my accident. It was the result of a broken world.

Finally, I pray that the story of this trial may move you to enliven your faith and make it stronger.

May you know God's path for you and follow it unswervingly.

May you love God more each day. Above all, may you trust in your Father, for you are his child.

Always know this:

God's purpose for you is great. Open your heart and your mind to his calling. Fulfill your purpose, and you, too, will be at peace.

Your servant,

William L. Kensey

CREDITS

Chapter 16 contains information and arguments consolidated, paraphrased and reformatted from portions of *The Creator and the Cosmos*, by Hugh Ross, PhD., Publisher: NavPress Publishing Group; Enlarged 3rd edition (Copyright June 1, 2001 by Reasons to Believe).

Made in the USA
Lexington, KY
07 January 2011